FRANK LLOYD WRIGHT

A GATEFOLD PORTFOLIO

TEXT BY

ROBIN LANGLEY SOMMER

PHOTOGRAPHS BY

BALTHAZAR KORAB

BARNES
& NOBLE
BOOKS
NEW YORK

Contents

INTRODUCTION

Frank Lloyd Wright was a remarkable draftsman who never started a drawing until he had the entire concept of a building clear in his mind. His colleague Bruce Brooks Pfeiffer recalls in the book *Frank Lloyd Wright Drawings* (Harry N. Abrams, Inc., in association with the Frank Lloyd Wright Foundation, 1990): "Perhaps the greatest value of his drawings lies in the fact that Wright loved to draw.... He was a swift draftsman—once the idea was clear in his mind, it came quickly onto paper. He maneuvered his T-square and triangle with a beautiful dexterity; it was a joy to watch him draw—to watch the lines appear so effortlessly."

Wright himself often referred to his pleasure in sitting down before a clean sheet of paper with his colored pencils and the other tools of his craft to sketch a new plan. Inspiration might strike at three o'clock in the morning and carry him into the daylight hours. And his enthusiasm was contagious, as seen in a talk that he gave to apprentices of the Taliesin Fellowship in 1955 (Frank Lloyd Wright Foundation Archives):

> All I can do is share that [experience] with the boys and girls who want to come in here, along a quest for something I myself haven't finished yet. You see, I am in it still, just the way you are. So is Olgivanna [his wife]. We are working and learning.... I think that this is the richest thing that could possibly have happened to us, that we have the opportunity to learn by way of your learning.

From the beginning, Wright had a sense of the value of his drawings to posterity. He began to save them as early as 1887, when he applied to Chicago architect Louis Sullivan for a position as draftsman. Fortunately, the early drawings survived several disastrous fires at his Wisconsin home and studio, Taliesin, in 1914 and 1925. Much later, he designated Taliesin West, in Scottsdale, Arizona, as the repository of his work.

FRANK LLOYD WRIGHT: A GATEFOLD PORTFOLIO

Much of our knowledge of Wright's drawings is due to architectural historian Bruce Brooks Pfeiffer, who studied with Wright and serves as director of the Frank Lloyd Wright Archives. As conservator, historian, and elucidator of Wright's work, he has done a major service not only to fellow architects, but to a general audience concerned with twentieth-century culture and design. Pfeiffer describes the various types of drawings involved in a project, from conceptual sketches and preliminary studies to presentation, development, and working drawings. (Few engineering drawings have been preserved, as they were sent to contractors on site.)

Most of the drawings in this portfolio are of the presentation type—detailed renderings shown to clients to sell the concept of a building. Wright's flair for drama and timing sped this process along. So did the handsome environments that established his credibility, from the serene octagonal library at his Oak Park, Illinois, studio to the beautiful complexes at Spring Green, Wisconsin, and Scottsdale, Arizona, each an integral part of its setting. The drawings speak for themselves. Designed to be easily read, they usually included a plan, or plans, if a second story is involved, and one or more perspectives. These presentation drawings give an impressive overview of the proposed building and include such details as foliage, flowers, color, and shading.

Not all of the drawings in this portfolio are from Wright's hand or his hand alone. In some cases, he prepared the conceptual sketches and the draftsmen made elevations or sections. In these cases, he usually did additional work on the rendering to bring it fully to life. The media employed included pencil and colored pencil; black, gold, and silver ink; watercolor and watercolor wash; and gouache.

Drawings from Wright's first period include the hundred plates prepared for the monograph of his work published in Berlin by Ernst Wasmuth in 1910. Its English title is *Executed Buildings and Projects*. Taylor Wooley and Wright's son, architect Lloyd Wright, collaborated on this work. Other members of the Oak Park studio staff also made major contributions, among them Marion Mahoney, Walter Burley Griffin, and Louis Rasmussen.

Gifted draftsmen employed during Wright's middle period (to 1931) include Heinrich Klumb, Donald Walker, and George Kastner. After the Taliesin Fellowship was founded in 1932, several dozen eager apprentices, some with previous experience in architecture, became part of Wright's extended household. A short list of these talented associates must include John Howe, John de Koven Hill, Stephen Oyakawa, Ling Po, and William Wesley Peters, who married Wright's stepdaughter, Svetlana.

From this point onward, it becomes easier to establish which draftsman worked on a given drawing; unsigned work was often attributed later on the basis of research.

The cleanly etched lines and meticulous shading of Wright's drawings show the influence of Japanese art, on which he was an authority. His collection of Japanese prints was one of the finest in the United States, and Oriental sculpture is a feature of his landscape and interior designs. His drawings, in turn, have been acquired by private collectors and museums, including New York City's Museum of Modern Art.

Former apprentices at Taliesin, including Pfeiffer and architect Donald W. Hoppen, have left vivid accounts of Wright's creative process. One story, recorded by Hoppen in *The Seven Ages of Frank Lloyd Wright: A New Appraisal* (Capra Press, 1993), tells of the plans for Wright's most famous house, Fallingwater. Wright had visited the western Pennsylvania site with the client, Edgar J. Kaufmann Sr., several months before, but nothing had appeared on the drawing board. The complex plan existed only in Wright's mind. When Kaufmann called to say that he was traveling in the area and would like to see the plans, Wright's apprentices were nervous. As Hoppen recalls it:

> With only a few hours left before Kaufmann was due, Wright sat down by the plot plan on the drafting board and began to draw. My friend, Edgar Tafel, was assisting apprentice, and describes the actual passage from Wright's imagination to the drawing board: "First floor plan. Second floor. Section, elevations. Side sketches of details, talking sotto voce all the while. The design just poured out of him.... Pencils being used up as fast as we could sharpen them when broken.... Erasures, overdrawing, modifying. Flipping sheets back and forth.... Then, the bold title across the bottom: *Fallingwater*. A house has to have a name."

After Kaufmann had seen the plan, which Hoppen describes as "breathtaking," Wright escorted him out to lunch so that the apprentices would have time to complete the other elevations.

Wright's love of drawing in the service of architecture and design is clear in the selections made for this portfolio from the more than 21,000 drawings that reside in the Frank Lloyd Wright Archives. They are a testimony to the towering achievement of a man who never spared himself in bringing into reality his vision of a new kind of architecture. ▣ ▣ ▣

FRANK LLOYD WRIGHT HOME AND STUDIO

OAK PARK, ILLINOIS (1889–1909)

Like so much of Wright's architecture, his first home/studio complex was constantly in the process of evolution. During the twenty-year period when he lived and worked here, his young family grew to include six children. The original two-story brick-and-shingle-surfaced house was modest in size but handsome and harmonious. It was enlarged in 1895 by the playroom addition, comprising a new kitchen and servants' room on the ground floor and the spacious barrel-vaulted children's playroom above. After 1898, when the studio was added, the extended household at 951 Chicago Avenue included half a dozen staff members during the day. At night, by his own account, Wright spent many hours in the studio sketching new plans and projects for his growing practice. He was a prodigious worker throughout his seventy-two-year career.

The Oak Park home and studio served as both laboratory and showcase for Wright's developing design principles. Although he maintained a Chicago office in the Rookery Building from 1898, much of his work was done for clients in Oak Park and the nearby suburb of River Forest. Thus, the studio, with its octagonal library, balconied drafting room, and terraced public entrance (added about 1906), not only gave form to his ideas but attracted new clients.

Many features characteristic of Wright's pioneering work in modern architecture, as detailed on the following page, are preserved at this site. It has been sensitively restored to its 1909 condition, the last year of Wright's residence, by the Frank Lloyd Wright Home and Studio Foundation. Now owned by the National Trust for Historic Preservation, the home and studio is one of seventeen structures designated by the American Institute of Architects to be retained as examples of Wright's architectural contribution to American culture. ▣ ▣ ▣

Playroom on second floor (Right)
Wright's romanticism had full scope in this vaulted room for his six children, located above the kitchen. Window seats overlook the garden as if from a tree house.

Stairway near home entrance, with Venus de Milo (Left)
A spindle screen of oak marks the landing, flowing into the other oak woodwork; it enriches the simple interior.

Dining room (Left, below)
Wright's famous high-backed chairs create an intimate area within the dining room, which was enlarged from the original kitchen in 1895. The wood ceiling grille conceals electric lights.

View of west facade, with home entrance (Below)
The shingle-style house was built in 1889 with a $5,000 loan from Wright's employer, Louis Sullivan. Some Oak Park neighbors considered it "seaside" or resort architecture of the kind then popular on the East Coast.

Frank Lloyd Wright Home and Studio

The home and studio at Oak Park are a kind of microcosm of Wright's formative years and nascent career. Characteristic features include disassembly of "the box," as he called the prevailing style, in favor of more open, flowing interior space; extended horizontal lines in the form of wood banding that forecast the emerging Prairie house; rhythmic bands of windows that provide ample light and a sense of connectedness to the outdoors; generous fireplace and chimney masses; and respectful use of natural and man-made materials, including brick, wood, concrete, metal, and glass.

The clean lines of the original gabled house owe much to Wright's 1886 apprenticeship as a draftsman to Joseph Lyman Silsbee, whose shingle-style buildings were influenced by the British architect Richard Norman Shaw. When Wright came to Chicago from his family home near Spring Green, Wisconsin, Silsbee had recently been commissioned by Wright's uncle, the Reverend Jenkin Lloyd Jones, to design a new church for his Unitarian congregation. Wright helped to design this modest brick-and-shingle structure, called Unity Chapel, which is within sight of the Taliesin Fellowship Complex at Spring Green.

A concomitant influence is that of the British Arts and Crafts movement, whose aesthetic was expressed by William Morris in the words, "Have nothing in your houses that you do not know to be useful, or believe to be beautiful." The *inglenook* (a recess with benches built beside a fireplace), surmounted by the motto "Truth Is Life," is typical of the Arts and Crafts movement. So is the use of art-glass windows and skylights, which contribute so much to the warmth of the interiors. Mellow burnished oak, subdued lighting fixtures, and "honest" workmanship throughout testify to the movement's influence on Wright's early designs.

The process of breaking down the square entailed an octagonal geometry expressed in the bay added to the north wall of the living room, the shape of the studio library, and the design for the drafting room, in which squares and octagons combine. The drafting room was the first of Wright's many open workspaces lighted from above, as would later be seen in the Larkin Company Administration Building of 1903 and the Johnson Wax Building of 1936.

The Oak Park home and studio help show the evolution of Wright's tendency to compress the space around entryways so as to heighten the sense of expectation about the interior. The doorway to the house is reached by shallow steps flanked by short piers and opens into a foyer of generous size. The living room is just left of the foyer and overlooks the brick-walled veranda. Privacy was an essential feature in Wright's residential designs. This may account in part for the addition of the complex public entrance to the studio, which was initially connected to the house by a passageway from the study. The new entrance, constructed about 1906, consisted of a low-walled terrace that gave access to the reception hall by way of a narrow covered portico at either end. The main activity space opens up as one enters the reception hall, lit by art-glass skylights of green, gold, and clear glass. The hall is serene and uncluttered, impressive but not imposing.

Initially, the house was furnished with antiques bought at local auctions. Then Wright began to design his own furniture, which he added to the interior along with built-in seating areas below the windows, upholstered in velvet, and an assortment of Oriental rugs. The diamond-panel *casement windows* (windows whose hinges are always attached to the upright side of the window-frame) predate the period when Wright began to design his own art glass. The recessed lighting behind the ceiling grille in the dining room is believed to be the first of its kind in this country.

Wright's affinity for bands of casement windows has much to do with their kinetic quality: They function as extended, mobile screens of glass, opening outward to the air and sunlight, as well as filtering light through their colored and patterned panes. The screen—of wood, glass, brick, concrete, or other material—would play a vital role in Wright's architecture, replacing walls and immovable partitions that block the free flow of space. His knowledge of Japanese art and architecture is apparent in the radical quality of his early work, which moved steadily away from conventional forms toward his expressed ideal that "form and function are one." Organic architecture, as he defined it, was not a fixed and final "product," but a process that would never be completed.

View of fireplace from living room (Above)

In the Arts and Crafts style, the inglenook with cushioned benches has a double brick fan around the fireplace with mottoes above.

Drafting room (Above)

Overhead lighting from fixtures of Wright's design supplements the natural lighting from clerestory windows at the balcony level. The balcony is suspended from a system of chains and pulleys.

Library (Right)

The octagonal library was added to the house along with the studio. Client presentations were made here in a setting that testifies to Wright's creativity.

View of north facade (Above)
Complete harmony was achieved
in integrating the additions to the
original six-room house.

Floor plan (Right)
First floor of home and studio, 1909,
with 1911 additions of garage and
caretaker's quarters, now a bookshop.

View of reception hall (Below)
The elegant reception hall, with
its rich bronze colors, is lighted
from above by three panels of gold
and green art glass.

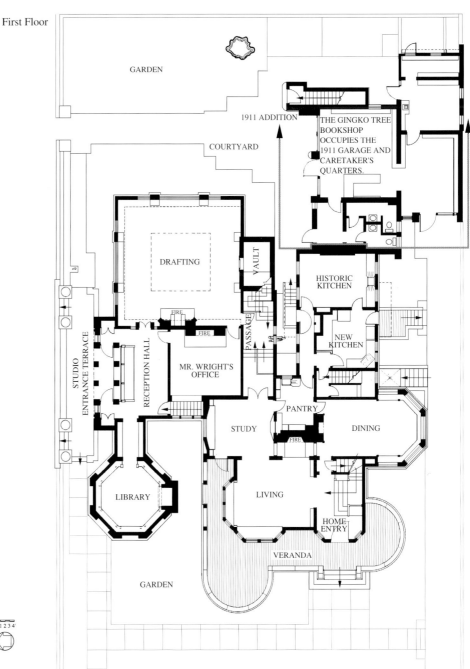

First Floor

GARDEN

1911 ADDITION

THE GINGKO TREE
BOOKSHOP
OCCUPIES THE
1911 GARAGE AND
CARETAKER'S
QUARTERS.

COURTYARD

DRAFTING

VAULT

HISTORIC
KITCHEN

FIRE

FIRE

PASSAGE

NEW
KITCHEN

STUDIO

ENTRANCE TERRACE

RECEPTION HALL

MR. WRIGHT'S
OFFICE

PANTRY

DINING

STUDY

FIRE

LIBRARY

LIVING

HOME
ENTRY

VERANDA

GARDEN

0 1 2 3 4'

Frank W. Thomas House

The residence built for Frank W. Thomas has been described as one of the great Prairie houses, and it has maintained that distinction through almost a hundred years of weathering, alteration, and restoration. One of more than forty houses designed by Wright in Oak Park, it was the first of its style, commissioned by James C. Rogers as a wedding present to his daughter and son-in-law.

The L-shaped plan of this Prairie-style house has been variously attributed to draftsmen Walter Burley Griffin and Marion Mahoney, both of whom worked in Wright's office and developed drawings for the Thomas house. In the absence of an excavated basement, the ground floor was designed with spacious servants' quarters; the raised main floor contains all the family living areas. The extended rooflines of the lower story project over the porch and the dining room at either end of the plan (overleaf). The top floor has four bedrooms in line, a bathroom, and storage space. Not seen in the rendering is a two-story addition at the back made in 1922 by Prairie school architects Thomas E. Tallmadge and Vernon S. Watson. Construction of the original house was of plaster on wood frame. The characteristically massive chimney was designed to ventilate the airspaces beneath the roofs in hot weather by means of openings that could be closed for the winter. It also served as a flue for the kitchen stove.

In the Thomas house, low horizontal lines, overhanging eaves, and the integration of site and structure combine to give the house a sense of shelter that prevails in almost all of Wright's residential designs. The off-center entrance is unusually complex. A walkway between high walls leads to the arched entryway. Within it are stairs to the left, a landing where the stairs reverse direction, and another ascent to a glazed breezeway at the second level. The sense of seclusion created by the Thomas house is reflected in its nickname, "The Harem." ▣ ▣ ▣

View of entry doors from hall *(Right, above)*

The extent and complexity of the art glass for the Thomas house was a significant factor in its cost. The view to the outside is left unobstructed by concentrating the pattern above and below the line of sight.

Detail of entry door *(Right)*

Current interest in Frank Lloyd Wright design elements has generated tasteful reproductions of selected art glass, furniture, lighting fixtures, and other objects that are as fresh today as at the turn of the century.

Frank W. Thomas House

ood banding occurs throughout the house, from the trim above the water table to the narrow horizontal strips at the top-floor level. Wood trim curves over the stuccoed entry arch, implying the presence of wood framing beneath the plaster facade. Inside, wood trim contributes to defining the free-flowing living spaces, including the breakfast alcove in the rectangular dining room to the right of the entry. The large rectangular living room has the hearth as its focal point and includes a book alcove defined by wood moldings that extend around the room and frame the art-glass casement windows.

The warm tones of wood and brick are complementary in the living room, where the low fireplace is set in a wide brick surround extending almost to ceiling height. Richly colored Oriental rugs bring out the golden tones of the oak flooring. The jewel-like colors of the windows and French doors work in harmony with these elements to create a comfortable interior very different from the fashionable Queen Anne and Tudor styles of the day.

The kitchen and pantries at the back of the house are large and well ventilated. Wright's objective of improving the quality of life for middle-class clients extended to their servants: He got them out of the traditional attics and basements and provided well-lighted working and living quarters in plans of this period. The smaller Usonian houses (an acronym for United States of North America) of his later career reflect the fact that live-in servants had become a rarity. Similarly, lot size and landscaping were scaled down as gardeners became a vanishing breed. Wright had a lifelong interest in moderate-cost housing, despite the fact that most of his clients were from the upper middle class, and many of them were very wealthy.

The Thomas house has many features in common with the larger Prairie house built for Ward Willits in nearby Highland Park at the same time. Neither house has a basement, and the first-floor living quarters are raised slightly above ground level. Both houses also have low-hipped roofs and horizontal banding on the exterior. The primary difference is the pinwheel plan for the latter house, which carries the sense of movement and continuity a step further, as the wings revolve from the central mass of the masonry fireplace. Both houses represent a radical change in American domestic architecture.

Front view by night (Left)
The strong horizontal planes of the
Thomas house stand out boldly below
the hovering masses of the rooflines.

View of entry from hall (Right)
The unusually complex entry route ends
in this elegant art-glass maze of doors
and panels. Their geometric pattern
recurs throughout the house.

**View of front facade
after restoration** (Below)
For many years, the house was covered
with shingles, totally compromising the
design. Fortunately, this condition was
corrected in 1975, when the original
plaster surface was restored.

Stairwell and entry porch (Left)
Unusually detailed woodwork at the entry porch has a circular motif contrasting with the rectangles and squares of the lamp and the art-glass panels in the doorway.

Ground-level entry (Right)
Masonry components of the Thomas house have suffered from weathering, especially the concrete water table here at the exterior-entry arch.

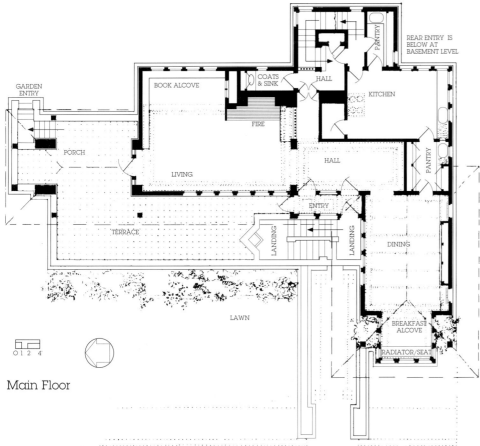

GARDEN ENTRY

BOOK ALCOVE

COATS & SINK

HALL

KITCHEN

REAR ENTRY IS BELOW AT BASEMENT LEVEL

PANTRY

FIRE

PORCH

LIVING

HALL

PANTRY

ENTRY

TERRACE

LANDING

LANDING

DINING

LAWN

BREAKFAST ALCOVE

RADIATOR/SEAT

0 1 2   4'

Main Floor

Terrace, with stairwell and entry porch (Below)
Ornamental newel posts with bead detailing, one of which carries a lighting fixture, flank the stairwell leading to the main entrance.

Floor plan (Above)
The main floor of the single-story wing contains the dining room, which has a gabled ceiling with wood bands and a large breakfast alcove.

Dana-Thomas House

Springfield, Illinois (1902)

As the rendering suggests, this house for heiress Susan Lawrence Dana was the largest that Wright had designed to that date. Originally planned as a remodeling and expansion of the client's existing Italianate house, it grew to include thirty-five rooms, three of them two stories high: the gallery, dining room, and reception hall.

Dana was an art collector and a well-known hostess of large social gatherings in the Illinois capital. The gallery was both a showcase and a reception room, connected to the house by a covered passage that doubled as a conservatory. The Prairie-style house has a cruciform plan, with all the principal common rooms on the first floor and bedrooms on the second. The basement of the original house was retained (despite Wright's aversion to basements) and enlarged to include a library, offices, a billiard room, and a bowling alley. Also retained was the original library on the first floor, converted into a parlor. It has a marble fireplace with a butterfly design that Wright adapted for the chandeliers in the dining room and gallery.

The principal naturalistic motif throughout the house derives from the prairie sumac. It appears as an abstract pattern in some 450 pieces of art glass, as well as rugs, murals, and other fixtures. Sculptor Richard Bock, artist George Niedecken, and the Linden Glass Company all collaborated on the project.

The house was purchased by Charles C. Thomas in 1944 and became the headquarters for his publishing firm, which was responsible for preserving the structure as Wright had built and furnished it. In 1976 the house was designated a National Historic Landmark. The State of Illinois bought the property in 1981 and undertook major restoration directed by Wilbert Hasbrouck of Hasbrouck Peterson Associates. ▣　▣　▣

Art-glass window, master bedroom (Below)

These east windows are part of a larger composition that includes the windows in the living room on the floor below.

Dining room, with entry hallway in background (Left)

The magnitude of the common areas is clear in this view of the barrel-vaulted dining room, with its hanging "butterfly" lamps and delicate mural of sumac and goldenrod by artist George Niedecken.

Gallery—facing north (Left), **facing south** (Right)

These views of the gallery, designed as a separate pavilion, suggest that large gatherings of the client's friends in artistic and political circles could be accommodated for the elaborate receptions she planned.

Dana-Thomas House

Wright's generous budget for the Dana house made it possible for him to include many features that contribute to its overall richness of color and form. The imposing facade has a Sullivanesque frieze of geometric forms in bronze green, with the angular prairie sumac as its central figure. Narrow Roman brick and stone are the principal building materials. The rooflines are low-pitched and upturned at the corners, suggesting the Japanese influence strikingly apparent in many of Wright's drawings. The decorative copper eaves and gutters have weathered to a green patina that harmonizes with the frieze.

The arched entryway flanked by blocky piers has a great fan of Roman brick: it has been described as

Wright's most beautiful arch. Above it, rectangular art-glass windows in autumnal colors provide filtered light to the two-story reception hall. Wright regarded the glass for this house as among his best efforts in the medium.

Numerous balconies overlook the grounds and the raised terrace on the street side of the house. Hanging plants once cascaded from the balconies and the large pedestal urns that Wright used so freely. (One client called them "those damned flowerpots.")

Inside, all the elements work together for a harmonious environment. The walls are of cream-colored brick and plaster; the woodwork is red oak. The high ceilings are sand-finished and the plaster walls textured and washed with color to create a subtle mottled effect. Solid oak furniture—more than a hundred pieces designed by Wright—echoes the finish and warm colors of the woodwork. The predominant colors throughout are gold, olive, orange, and red.

The two-story dining room, with its barrel-vaulted ceiling, was designed to seat up to forty guests. At one end is a deep bay with built-in seating for more intimate groupings. Such nooks and alcoves are found throughout the house. The upper walls of the dining room carry a mural of delicate foliage painted by George Niedecken, who also collaborated on the elegant Meyer May house in Grand Rapids, Michigan (1908). The complex art-glass lamps suspended above the dining table were sketched by Wright in 1900. The Frank Lloyd Wright Foundation archives also contain sketches for copper vases, bronze urns, and hanging stained-glass screens for the Dana house.

Sculptor Richard Bock, who contributed to Wright's Oak Park home and studio, was called upon to integrate works of art into the large public spaces of the Dana house. His sculpture titled "The Flower in the Crannied Wall" stands in the entry near the terra-cotta fountain, which he also designed. The fortunate combination of a sensitive client, gifted collaborators, and an ample budget helped Wright make this house a landmark of modern architecture.

Exterior view of entrance (Left)
The entryway has an imposing double brick fan, flanking piers, and an art-glass fanlight in a butterfly motif.

Art-glass window, sumac motif (Below)
This is one of some 450 pieces of art glass in the house related to the abstracted design of a prairie sumac.

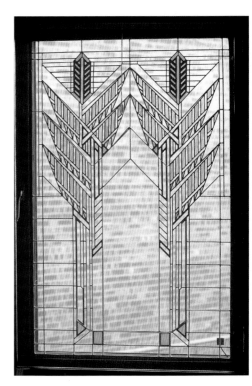

Detail of the west facade (Below)
The plaster frieze reflects the influence of Louis Sullivan, Mr. Wright's mentor.

Detail of art-glass windows (Far left)
Gold and amber predominate in these intricate windows, made to Wright's design, like all the glasswork in the house, by the Linden Glass Company of Chicago.

Reception area (Above)
This house contained Wright's first multistory rooms, including this complex reception hall, which soars past the balcony level and extends horizontally north to the parlor (called the Victorian Room) and west from the living area to the conservatory.

Perspective view of south facade (Left)
The prominent entrance of the Dana-Thomas house is unlike most of Wright's houses, which typically have entries that are not so easily accessible from the street.

Floor plan (Below)
The extensive floor plan for this complex house indicates that price was no object to Susan Lawrence Dana in realizing the mansion she asked Wright to create from what he called the "old homestead" (the original Lawrence house).

First Floor

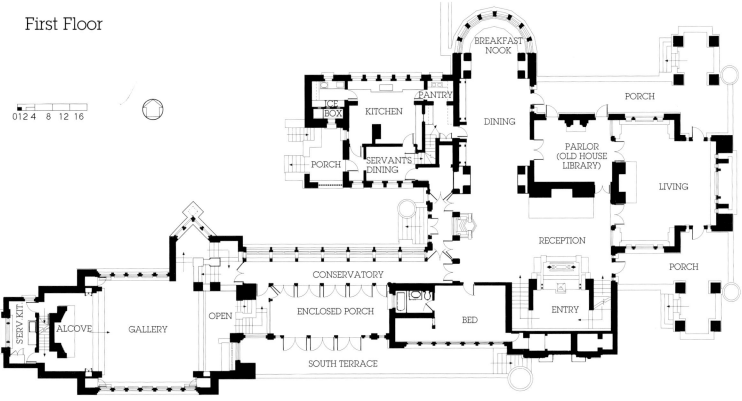

012 4   8   12 16

BREAKFAST NOOK

ICE BOX   KITCHEN   PANTRY

PORCH

DINING

PORCH

SERVANTS DINING

PARLOR (OLD HOUSE LIBRARY)

LIVING

RECEPTION

PORCH

SERV. KIT.

ALCOVE   GALLERY   OPEN

CONSERVATORY

ENCLOSED PORCH

BED

ENTRY

PORCH

SOUTH TERRACE

East facade (Left)
This view shows how the gabled roofline — atypical of Wright's hipped-roof plan — makes the three-story facade appear even taller than it is.

Unity Temple

Oak Park, Illinois (1904)

Wright's first ecclesiastical commission, this massive four-square structure of concrete was originally known as Unity Church. Over time, Wright's name for the worship space, Unity Temple—the north section—was applied to the whole building, which includes the parish hall—Unity House, on the south side—and a central entrance *loggia* (a gallery that is open on one or more sides). It was commissioned by the Unitarian Universalist Church in Oak Park, a congregation of some 400 members with a modest budget.

In design and material, this was a radical innovation in church architecture. In his text for the Wasmuth portfolio of his early works, published in Germany in 1910, Wright described the building as "a concrete monolith cast in wooden forms, exterior surfaces washed clean to expose the small gravel aggregate, the finished result not unlike a coarse granite." (Later, the surface was coated with gunite, a concrete mixture sprayed from a special gun that effectively obliterated the pour lines in the cast-concrete forms.)

From the low *plinth* (the projecting base of the wall) that Wright consistently used as a foundation during this period, the building rises to the slab roof of waterproof concrete jutting out over the rectangular masses of the walls.

The three-level floor plan on the following page delineates the piers at the corners of the worship space, which house the stairways. The loggia connecting church and parish hall is reached by a terrace, and the rectangular hall comprises classrooms, kitchen, and space for social activities. Wright reported that his biggest challenge was the integration of worship and social areas—a process that required more than thirty-three studies.

The building is one of seventeen structures designated by the American Institute of Architects to be retained as examples of Wright's architectural contribution to American culture. ▣ ▣ ▣

View of balconies
and ceiling *(Right, above)*

The balconies provide adequate seating within the sanctuary; they are lighted from above by bands of clerestory windows and coffered skylights.

Floor plan *(Left)*

Composite plan of three levels: Imaginative use of the limited space on the building site provided ample accommodations for the 400-member congregation in both the sanctuary and the parish hall.

Interior view *(Right)*

Most critics consider this sanctuary, cleanly defined by slender wood banding and overhung by graceful fixtures of Wright's design, one of his highest achievements.

UNITY TEMPLE

Unity Temple was a landmark not only in church architecture, but in Wright's career, as he stated on several occasions. One of them was the first in a series of four lectures delivered in London in 1939 at the invitation of the Royal Institute of British Architects. Referring to the concept of organic architecture, which was rooted in antiquity, he told the audience of young architects that "the first building which I consciously built as an honest endeavor on my part to express this 'new' idea of building was Unity Temple." Later, in 1952, he reiterated that statement in these words: "Unity Temple is where you will find the first real expression of the idea that the space within the building is the reality of that building"—a concept that had been articulated by the Chinese philosopher Lao-tzu 2,400 years earlier.

Wright's long love affair with the possibilities of concrete as a building material began here and continued in such diverse expressions as Chicago's Midway Gardens (1913); the Kaufmann residence, Fallingwater, at Mill Run, Pennsylvania (1935); and New York City's Guggenheim Museum (1956). The attractions of concrete include plasticity, durability, and economy, all of which figured in Wright's choice of this material for Unity Temple, which was the first reinforced-concrete structure on this scale in the United States. As Terry L. Patterson

observes in *Frank Lloyd Wright and the Meaning of Materials* (Van Nostrand Reinhold, 1994): "Concrete offered to Wright, in one material, the structural freedom afforded by the great strength of steel and the true plasticity inherent in casting. These qualities, combined with the neutral personality that he observed in its surface and the lack of a traditional image, provided to Wright the greatest opportunity among his materials to define a material's nature without interference from external influences."

Both parts of the building are lighted by bands of leaded-glass *clerestory windows* (windows that pierce the upper main walls) and by amber skylights worked into the *coffered ceiling* (a decorative ceiling of sunken ornamental panels). Organ, choir loft, and pulpit form a tripartite arrangement whereby the presider is in close proximity to the congregation, fostering a sense of intimacy impossible to achieve with the conventional raised pulpit. The sanctuary inscribes a Greek cross in a square. Ornamental impressions were cast integrally with the columns along the facade.

Restoration of the building began in 1969 and was expedited by a fire in Unity House in 1971 that necessitated extensive repair. Subsequent work has been carried out under the auspices of the Unity Temple Restoration Foundation, formed in 1973, which prepared a Historic Structures Report. Unity Temple is still owned and occupied by the spiritual community that commissioned the building after the turn of the century.

Enclosure of the stairwells of the sanctuary in the corner piers makes the balconies a series of floating bridges, defined but not limited by the rectangular wood banding that extends into the coffered ceiling, with its recessed skylights. Thus, the horizontal flow of the balconies moves, in turn, into the vertical *fenestration* (the arrangement of windows) of the stained-glass clerestory windows, to create a continuous plane of light and space. Fixed furnishings, including the suspended lighting fixtures, reprise the theme of the Greek cross formed by the extended roofline. Unity Temple's sanctuary remains a major achievement almost a hundred years after it was designed.

FOR THE WORSHIP OF GOD
AND THE SERVICE OF MAN

View of pulpit, with stairways to choir and loggia (Below)
The sense of relatedness between minister and congregation is enhanced by the projection of the pulpit into the worship space.

Perspective view of west facade (Right)
The cement construction of Unity Temple insulated the congregation from the noise of the trolley line that ran nearby in the early 1900s.

Exterior view of temple (Above)
Wright described Unity Temple as "a concrete monolith cast in wooden forms,… the finished result not unlike a coarse granite." The surface has been refinished to obliterate the original pour lines.

Detail of exterior columns (Far left)
Essentially a composition of rectangular masses, Unity Temple has little ornamentation apart from the geometric designs precast in the concrete columns of the facade.

**Exterior view of facade,
facing terrace** (Right)
The terrace between the church and the
social center, Unity House, provides
access to the central entry hall.

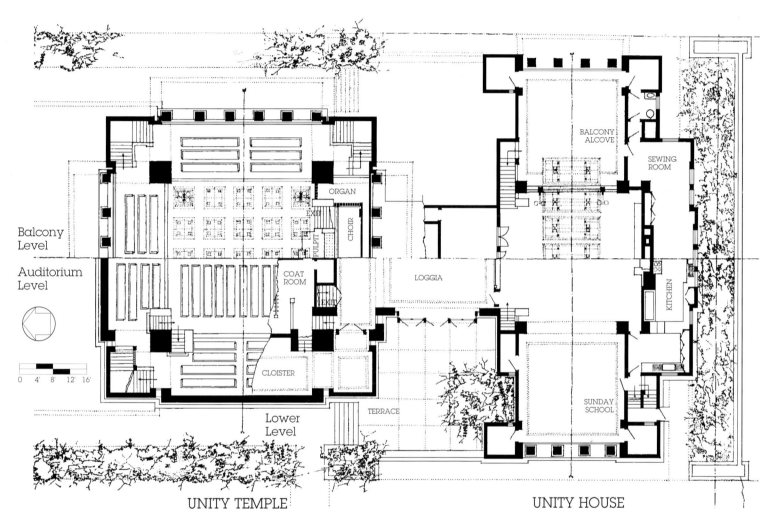

Balcony
Level

Auditorium
Level

0 4' 8' 12' 16'

ORGAN

EXIT

PULPIT

CHOIR

COAT
ROOM

EXIT

LOGGIA

CLOISTER

BALCONY
ALCOVE

SEWING
ROOM

KITCHEN

SUNDAY
SCHOOL

Lower
Level

TERRACE

UNITY TEMPLE

UNITY HOUSE

View of west facade (Left)
The flat projecting roofs, of waterproof
reinforced concrete, form a Greek cross
above the cubical sanctuary, contributing
to the monolithic presence of the building.

Frederick C. Robie House

Chicago, Illinois (1906)

The best-known of all Wright's Prairie houses was not built in the suburbs, but on a narrow corner lot in Chicago. Its streamlined design, years ahead of its time, led German critics to call it *Dampfer,* or steamship, architecture. The house was commissioned by a successful young inventor who asked Wright to incorporate the newest technology in his design for a contemporary house that had everything in it, from furnishings to modern utilities. Robie himself contributed to the plans for the telephone, electrical installations, and vacuuming system.

As seen in the perspective drawing, the Robie house extends along a single horizontal axis under cantilevered roofs that seem to hover above the structure, extending outward as much as twenty feet from their masonry supports. Roman brick and limestone, free of ornamentation, are the visible construction materials, used to form blocky masses and piers. Consistent with Wright's usual practice, there is no excavated basement. The ground-floor level was designed to contain a playroom, a billiard room, utility areas, and an entirely new feature: a garage integral to the house. This garage and its surrounding wall were altered after the Robies left the property.

The flow of interior space is unbroken in the principal common areas of the raised main floor. The massive fireplace serves as a screen rather than a divider between the living and dining areas, each of which ends in a diamond-shaped bay overlooking the porch and the drive, respectively. Kitchen and servants' quarters were grouped at the rear of the main floor. The third floor housed family and guest bedrooms and baths. Extensive screens of art-glass windows and French doors provide both light and privacy.

The Frederick C. Robie house is one of seventeen structures designated by the American Institute of Architects to be retained as examples of Wright's architectural contribution to American culture. ▣ ▣ ▣

Detail, living room windows (Above)
The principal motif in the windows for this house (this is one of four different patterns) is an abstraction of natural plant forms from the prairie, which was still visible from this site when the Robie house was built.

Living room, with fireplace (Above)
The Robie house was revolutionary in having no walls or partitions to block the flow of space through the family living areas. The fireplace serves as a screen, and the custom-designed rug unifies the entire space.

View of southeast facade (Below)
Providing both access to the outdoors and total privacy, the porches and balconies resemble the various decks of a ship, which served as the model for the totally innovative plan.

Frederick C. Robie House

The antecedent of the Robie house appears in a pencil perspective sketched by Wright in 1904, when he designed a similar Prairie house for the Frederick F. Tomeks in Riverside, Illinois. Wright historian William Allin Storrer states in *The Frank Lloyd Wright Companion* (University of Chicago Press, 1993) that "the later designed and built Robie is a mirror image of the Tomek in all basic elements of design." The two houses share features including: long, extended lines; cantilevered roofs, the thrust of which is empha-sized by short, nonsupporting piers below; and a central stairwell ascending through all three floors. A major difference in the Robie house is in the placement of the entry, which is not even visible from the street. Access is at the ground-floor level in back of the house. Another innovation is the south facade on the main level, where a continuous band of art-glass doors reaching to the eaves overlooks a shallow balcony. Their geometric design, based on abstract plant forms, is one of four reprised throughout the house. The predominant color is gold, harmonizing with the furniture and fixtures, all of which, including the carpets, were designed by Wright and his associates.

The main level of the Robie house is unique for its time in having no walls or partitions to interrupt the space of the common areas. The chimney between living and dining rooms is divided into two flues, one on each side of the recessed hearths, which are positioned back to back. This leaves the space above mantel level open to a continuous view of the wood-banded ceiling, which extends into the upper walls to support spherical lighting fixtures. The high-backed chairs around the dining room table create the sense of a smaller enclosure within the room, as do the lighting piers at the corners of the table, seen also at the Meyer May house in Grand Rapids, Michigan.

The oak furniture has the same finish and trim as the wall and ceiling moldings. It includes an unusual sofa with slightly flared legs and wide table arms, square coffee tables and stools with flared legs, and the dining room chairs with their vertical slats, similar to those made for the Oak Park home/studio. Artist George Niedecken coordinated the Robie house interiors; his wife, a gifted seamstress, may have worked on the geometric designs for the woven carpets.

Built at a cost of sixty thousand dollars—prohibitive at the time—the Robie house has become a National Historic Landmark. Called "the house of the century" by *House and Home* magazine in 1958, it is now owned by the University of Chicago.

Living room windows, west end (Right)
Many of the small panes in the masterful leaded-glass windows are iridescent; the colors gold and amber predominate.

View of entrance court on north facade (Far left)
A low wall frames the entrance court, paved in concrete with a central inset of red quarry tiles. Steps rise behind a brick pylon to the west porch.

Robie wall lamp (Below)
The elegant brass wall lamps comprise a circle within a square (one of Wright's favorite geometric configurations). It is reprised on the terrace in the form of pedestal flower urns.

Dining room, looking east (Above)
Consistent with the living room, the dining room also has its "prow;" though here it serves as breakfast alcove as well. The oak chairs with their tall backs create a sense of intimacy for those dining at the table.

Stairwell (Left)
Located directly behind the living room fireplace, the handsome stairwell ascends from the entrance hall to the second (main) floor.

Perspective view of south facade

(Left)

Recessed between the brick piers of this south exposure are twelve pairs of art-glass French doors running the entire length of the living/dining areas. The streamlined, shiplike profile of the house set it apart from the traditional three-story houses in this Chicago neighborhood.

Second (Main) Floor

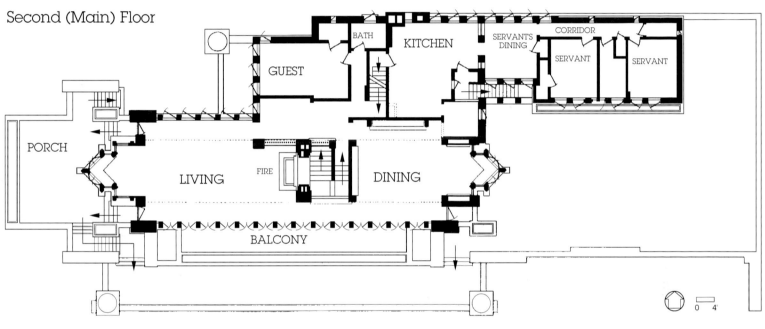

Floor plan *(Above)*

The shiplike profile of the Robie house is clear in this plan of the main level, which shows the "prows" jutting out at each end of the living/dining area (the "main vessel"), while the kitchen and adjacent rooms occupy the "service vessel" at the rear of the house.

Living room, looking west *(Right)*

In the diamond-shaped bay, called a prow, are ten casement windows and two flanking doors wrought of colored glass, which casts a rich tapestry of light into the room.

John Storer House

Hollywood, California (1923)

Wright made a pencil study for a concrete-block house in southern California as early as 1921, but the prototype of the four textile-block houses he built during this period was not constructed until 1923. This was the Alice Madison Millard house in Pasadena, closely followed by the monumental three-story house for Los Angeles client John Storer. Both were built of precast concrete blocks impressed with patterns of Wright's design by wood and metal molds, respectively. The result was a richly textured surface both on the interior and exterior walls, which were constructed with an airspace between them. Wright called this building system "textile block" because the parallel rows of four-inch-thick blocks were knitted together by steel rods, horizontally and vertically.

A stepped-back plan on three levels gives the Storer house, on its steep hillside, a commanding presence and a panoramic view of Los Angeles. The house has a flat roof and two wings, joined at entry level by a formal dining room off the reception area. The plan is unusual in that the high-ceilinged living room is on the top floor. It opens to a terrace at either end and is lighted by the tall, narrow windows between the columns of the facade along both sides of the room. This facade of glass and concrete is continuous with that of the dining room below.

Furniture for this house was not custom designed: the present owner has furnished it with an eclectic blend of Wright and Arts and Crafts objects and ornaments from his extensive collection. During the 1980s, the building was fully restored by Joel Silver and architect Eric Wright, the grandson of Frank Lloyd Wright. ▣ ▣ ▣

Living room (Left)
Filtered sunlight burnishes the rich red and gold woodwork of the two-story living room, embellished by sculpture and pottery on a large scale in keeping with that of the house.

Pool on north terrace (Below)
The restoration undertaken by Joel Silver in 1980, with Eric Wright as architect, brought the Storer house back to its original 1920s splendor. The north terrace was previously a sunken garden.

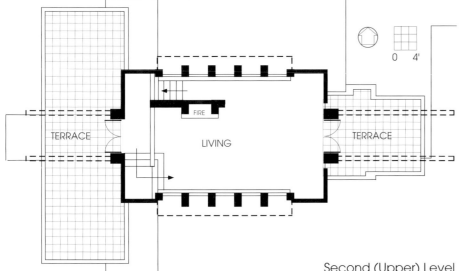

0   4'

TERRACE   LIVING   TERRACE

FIRE

Second (Upper) Level

JOHN STORER HOUSE

The Storer house is one of about sixty Wright buildings made of concrete block, or with major elements of block construction. It employs three types of concrete blocks cast on the site: plain, patterned, and pierced. The flexibility of this material over other forms of masonry, including brick and stone, was one of its major attractions for the architect.

The house has alternating rows of plain and patterned concrete blocks. The two-story columns along the upper level are made of paired half-blocks alternating vertically; half-blocks are also used as *copings* (a capping on the exterior walls to throw off rain or snow). The stepped-back and stacked elements contribute to the rhythmic flow of the design from the walled terraces at the base to the *fasciae* (normally, horizontal bands at the roofline with moldings, but in this case without).

The textile-block houses have been variously described as pre-Columbian, neo-Gothic, and Middle Eastern in effect. In fact, they are a unique synthesis of Wright's views on organic architecture in the Machine Age. Ancient architects could not have used masonry in this way because of the technology involved, yet that technology has been used to create a fresh work imprinted by an artist's hand. As Terry L. Patterson points out in *Frank Lloyd Wright and the Meaning of Materials* (Van Nostrand Reinhold, 1994): "Although Wright promoted the machine as an appropriate influence in architecture, he also held the scope of its influence to be a matter of judgment. 'Repetition carried beyond a certain point,' he wrote [in *Architectural Record*, 1927], 'has always taken the life of anything addressed to the living spirit.'"

The rich ornamentation intrinsic to this textile-block house, so ideally suited to its setting, has been enhanced by the addition of native plants. The house was landscaped by Lloyd Wright, who also supervised its construction during his father's extended absences in Japan to fulfill the Imperial Hotel commission. The south exposure overlooks the pond and entry, and extensive plantings were designed for the lower-level terraces. The original sunken garden beside the north terrace has been modified by a swimming pool.

It is certain that Wright would have continued his experiments in textile-block construction had the Depression not intervened. Lack of money and materials closed the period of what he called his Romanzas.

Second-floor hallway (Far left)
The Storer house resembles a movie set in this imposing view of the two-story hallway, with alternating concrete block and glass along the exterior wall.

West terrace, off living room (Below)
Outdoor living space is one of the most attractive features of this successful California house. Lloyd Wright designed the landscaping.

View of living room (Right)
A low hearth in the block chimney is the focal point for a grouping of contemporary furniture that harmonizes with the setting. Wright did not design the Storer house furniture.

South terrace entry (Left)
Four different block designs, several of which are seen here at the entrance, combine harmoniously both on the exterior and interior walls. Simple art-glass panels frame the doorway.

South terrace (Right)
The water garden offers a pleasing contrast to the textured masonry of the south terrace, which overlooks the Los Angeles valley.

View of south facade *(Right)*
*Mysterious but accessible, the
house blends beautifully with its
hillside setting, now filled with
mature plantings.*

Floor plan *(Left)*
*The entry-level plan makes it clear that
privacy was effectively protected by
extensive plantings and terraces around
the living quarters.*

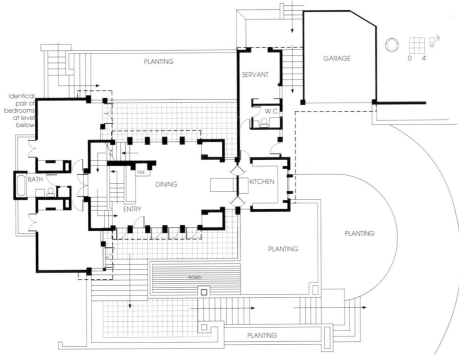

Main (Entry/Lower) Level

Floor plan *(Right)*
*Plan of second (upper) level, showing
terraces at either end of the living room:
Wright described the Storer house as
"a pre-fabricated mono-material house
eliminating skilled labor in its
construction." Even so, cost overruns
were prohibitive.*

ENNIS-BROWN HOUSE

LOS ANGELES, CALIFORNIA (1923)

The Ennis-Brown house has undergone many changes during its seventy-year history, but it retains the massive linear quality seen in the original perspective. The other three textile-block houses of this period were much smaller and fostered a sense of enclosure and repose. In 1954 Wright himself admitted that he had exceeded the limits of his material in the Ennis house, "which was way out of concrete-block size. I think that was carrying it too far—that's what you do, you know, after you get going, and get going so far that you get out of bounds."

The present perspective (right) shows the monumental scale of the Ennis house, the largest of the four concrete-block houses built for California clients during the mid-1920s. As seen most clearly at left, the retaining wall forms a major part of the house, which is constructed of plain and patterned concrete blocks joined by steel rods in the building system Wright called "textile block." The small dimensions of the blocks made it possible to follow the contours of the site closely. The Ennis house overlooks Los Angeles from a spur of the Santa Monica Mountains.

A colonnade of the same patterned blocks used for the exterior frames the principal indoor and outdoor living spaces. The blocks were cast on the site, and Wright included decomposed local granite in the concrete mix for its color value. Unfortunately, this had an adverse effect on durability: large sections of the south retaining wall collapsed during the 1980s. The Ennis house changed hands half a dozen times before Mr. and Mrs. August Brown bought it in 1968. They undertook much-needed restoration work before turning it over to the Trust for Preservation of Cultural Heritage, created by Brown to maintain the house for the future. His contribution is recognized in the change of name to the Ennis-Brown house. ▣ ▣ ▣

Interior view *(Left)*
The contrast between plain and patterned blocks makes a richly textured, rhythmic pattern of verticals and horizontals rising two stories.

View of living room and dining room *(Left, below)*
The large common areas are richly appointed in teak, marble, and bronze in accordance with the demands of the client, Charles Ennis, who lived in the house until his death at the age of seventy.

View of east facade *(Below)*
When it was built in the early 1920s, this largest of the textile-block houses cost $150,000 (a prohibitive sum for the time).

ENNIS-BROWN HOUSE

Despite its great size, the Ennis house, built on several levels, has comparatively few rooms, as seen in the floor plan (right). Originally, two bedrooms were separated by a terrace and connected to the common areas by a long gallery overlooking the north terrace. Adjacent living and dining rooms ended at the kitchen, pantry, and guest room. Entry is below the main level, from a large courtyard with garage and chauffeur's quarters at one end. Much of the structure comprises terraces and stairways to the various levels. The interior is lofty and formal, recalling the great hall of a Gothic castle.

During Wright's long absences at Taliesin, his son, architect Lloyd Wright, dealt with the many difficulties posed by the steep site and the demands of the client, Charles Ennis. He prepared the working drawings, supervised construction, and designed the landscaping in keeping with the arid climate.

Wright's designs for the art-glass clerestory windows in this house—an abstract pattern of the flowering wisteria vine—were his last for residential use. The wisteria pattern is reprised in a golden Tiffany mosaic over the hall fireplace. Many of the decorative elements were installed by the Ennises in expensive materials, including teak (used for the woodwork), bronze, and marble. There was a total rupture between client and architect before the house was completed. In this case, Wright's charm failed him.

The patterned blocks used inside and out have the same orientation: most face one way, rather than alternate with pierced blocks, as in the Storer house (following page), or occur in pairs. This contributes to the monumental quality of the Ennis-Brown house, which has been compared to a Mayan temple. When the blocks were stacked to form pillars, as in the colonnade, their lack of uniformity made them hard to align. In the absence of mortar joints, the hollows inside were filled with grout or concrete to add strength. Another problem common to many of Wright's other designs was a leaking roof, which numerous owners of this Los Angeles house had to contend with before it was corrected.

During World War II, the house was purchased by radio personality John Nesbitt, who retained Wright to add a swimming pool on the north terrace, a billiard room on the ground floor, and a heating system. When the Browns took occupancy, they replaced one bedroom and bath with a Japanese garden opposite the pool.

Wright had foreseen the impact of the Machine Age on architecture even before he delivered his famous lecture titled "The Art and Craft of the Machine" at Chicago's Hull House in 1901. However, it was not until the 1920s that he constructed entire buildings from prefabricated, mass-produced modules—the textile-block houses. It was a bold and largely successful experiment that gave impetus to such later achievements as the campus for Florida Southern College in Lakeland (1938–54).

View of surrounding landscape
(Left)

Crowning a ridge in the Santa Monica Mountains, the monumental Ennis-Brown house looks more like a public building than a private residence. The massive south retaining wall has been compromised by weathering.

Detail of concrete block (Below)

This complex geometric design recalls the masonry of a Mayan temple, to which the house has often been compared.

Wrought-iron grillwork (Above)

This intricate metal screen overlooks the colonnade of the main living area.

Interior view of entry hall fireplace (Left)

Framed by massive columns, the fireplace is surmounted by a golden Tiffany mosaic of wisteria. The design for the mosaic is abstracted in the art-glass clerestory windows.

View of north facade (Right)

These walls, facing away from Los Angeles, are relatively free of damage from the 1994 earthquake and the effects of pollution.

View of south facade (Left)

A long loggia on the north side of the house connects two bedrooms with a terrace between them. Surprisingly for its size, the house has only six rooms.

Floor plan (Below)

The plan of the upper levels of the main house and chauffeur's quarters shows that the majority of the space on the building site was given over to walled terraces, court-yards, and garden enclosures for outdoor living in the congenial California climate.

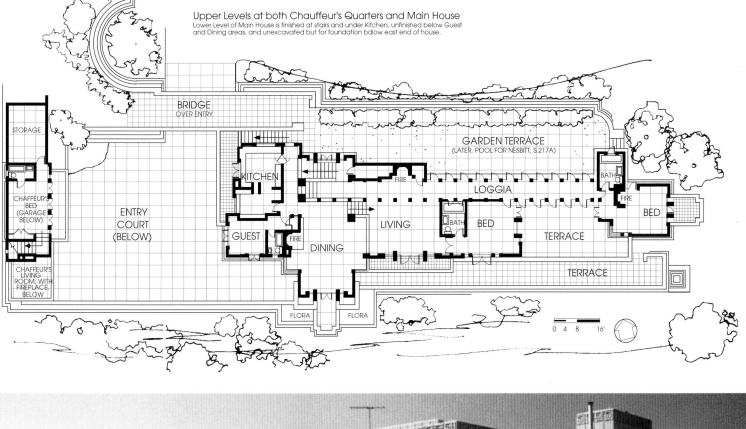

Upper Levels at both Chauffeur's Quarters and Main House
Lower Level of Main House is finished at stairs and under Kitchen, unfinished below Guest and Dining areas, and unexcavated but for foundation below east end of house.

STORAGE

CHAUFFEUR'S BED (GARAGE BELOW)

CHAUFFEUR'S LIVING ROOM, WITH FIREPLACE, BELOW

BRIDGE OVER ENTRY

ENTRY COURT (BELOW)

KITCHEN

GUEST

FIRE

DINING

LIVING

GARDEN TERRACE
(LATER, POOL FOR NESBITT, S.217A)

FIRE

LOGGIA

BATH

BED

BATH

FIRE

BED

TERRACE

TERRACE

FLORA   FLORA

0 4 8   16'

Taliesin Fellowship Complex (Hillside)

Spring Green, Wisconsin (1932)

Generations of family history have been impressed upon the rural landscape where Wright established his second home/studio (1911) and, in 1932, the Taliesin Fellowship. The property came to him through his mother, Anna Lloyd Jones, and grew to include two earlier buildings of his own design, commissioned by his aunts Nell (Ellen) and Jane Lloyd Jones. The first was the innovative windmill he called Romeo and Juliet (1896), a sixty-foot tower combining octagonal- and diamond-shaped forms that supported each other. The windmill supplied water to the second structure, Hillside Home School II (1902), a progressive coeducational boarding school founded by his aunts. The school had outgrown its original shingle-style building, designed by Wright in 1887; the second building was completed in 1903.

In 1933 the building was remodeled, as described on the following page, into the Taliesin Fellowship complex, where apprentices in architecture studied under Wright. Hillside, as it is now called, has been a creative force in architecture and design for almost seventy years. Other additions and expansions for the complex, shown on the accompanying rendering, were never realized.

On the other side of the hill is the Midway Farm complex and the beautiful house and studio Wright called Taliesin, invoking from his Welsh heritage the name that means "shining brow." Begun in 1911, it has been rebuilt twice after major fires and has grown from its original 7,000 square feet to five times that size, excluding gardens, terraces, and courtyards. The low, sheltering buildings of native limestone are connected by roofed passageways and courts.

Taliesin I, so called to distinguish it from Taliesin West in Scottsdale, Arizona, is one of seventeen structures designated by the American Institute of Architects to be retained as examples of Wright's architectural contribution to American culture. ▣　▣　▣

Romeo and Juliet Windmill (Above)
Wright's Lloyd Jones relatives predicted
that his unusual windmill would blow
down in the first strong gale, but his engineering has withstood the test since 1896.

Hillside Studio (Below)
Bold triangles define the great
workspace created in the north end of
the original school building in 1932 and
refurbished in 1978–80.

Taliesin Fellowship Complex (Hillside)

The principal material of this building is rose-colored sandstone that encloses a vertical space in the form of a three-story assembly room. This room, in turn, is linked by a classroom-lined gallery to the balconied gymnasium on the west side. A bridge-gallery over the driveway connected this part of the building to the rooms north of the assembly hall, forming two cruciform units.

At the age of sixty-five, when most people are retiring, Wright opened his school for architecture and the allied arts with the help of his third wife, Olgivanna. Born in Montenegro, she had studied at the Gurdjieff Institute at Fontainebleau and was as progressive in her views on education as Wright himself.

The venue for this new venture was the Hillside Home School, which would be remodeled extensively over a period of years to accommodate the young people who came to Taliesin as apprentices. Some were housed at the home/studio, others in dormitories converted from classrooms at Hillside. The gymnasium of the former school became the Hillside Playhouse, rebuilt as the Hillside Theatre after a fire in 1952. A large drafting studio flanked by apprentice rooms was added to the north section of the existing building, which had housed laboratory classrooms. This space was renovated in the late 1970s and now serves as headquarters for Taliesin Architects Ltd.

As shown on overleaf, Wright's initial plans for the complex envisioned additional buildings and expansions that were never realized due to financial constraints. Similarly, Midway Farm, which was planned to make the Fellowship largely self-sustaining in food production, could not be operated on a scale large enough to realize this objective.

The first nineteen apprentices arrived in October 1932 and became involved in all the activities of the 200-acre property, from cutting stone to building ponds, making furniture, and raising crops. Music, drama, and cinema were important components of the community's social and intellectual life. In the revised prospectus published by the Taliesin Fellowship in December 1933, Wright described the community's activities and objectives: "Fundamental architecture is the first essential of organic living and fruitful culture in this work at Taliesin. The generation of life and art alike cannot be taught, only experienced....The integrity of this architecture is an important feature in the life of the Fellowship, and although many of the buildings are completed or are well along, every apprentice will have a share in extending the group of buildings."

After the Hillside Playhouse was destroyed by fire in 1952, Wright designed a new theater with its own foyer and created a dining room overlooking the stage from balcony level. In the great drafting room, he and the apprentices worked on the concept and model for Broadacre City—a decentralized urban/suburban complex that would never be fully realized. However, it did exert a compelling influence on city planners and future architects as well as on the Usonian houses of the years 1936 onward.

Hillside Theatre (Above)
Members of the Taliesin Fellowship enjoyed films, plays, and lectures in the colorful contemporary theater constructed by Wright in 1952.

Fu Dog sculpture at entrance to Taliesin I (Left)
This is one of many Oriental artworks at Wright's beautiful Wisconsin home and studio, originally constructed in 1911. He had a deep appreciation for Eastern art. His collection of Japanese prints was of the highest quality.

Courtyard at Taliesin I (Above)
The house seems to grow from its site, because the limestone walls were laid up to resemble natural outcroppings of the native stone.

Entrance to Midway Farm (Left)
Starting in the early 1930s, the farm produced much of the community's food.

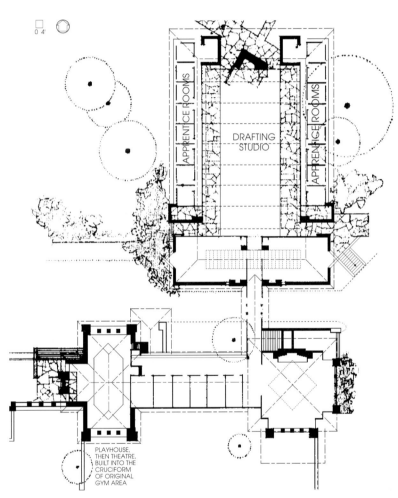

APPRENTICE ROOMS

APPRENTICE ROOMS

DRAFTING STUDIO

PLAYHOUSE, THEN THEATRE, BUILT INTO THE CRUCIFORM OF ORIGINAL GYM AREA

View of south facade of Hillside
(*Above*)

Theater and dining room: The theater was designed to be overlooked by the dining room, which is at balcony level to the stage. This facility replaced the earlier playhouse, which was destroyed by fire.

Hillside dining room (*Right*)

A rare example of a gabled dining room by Wright, this was adapted from former classroom space in the building he had designed for his aunts. It overlooks the theater's stage from behind.

Floor plan (*Left*)

Elements of the original Hillside Home School designed in 1902 can be traced in this Hillside Complex plan for adaptation of the school to the needs of the Fellowship. Rooms shown here between the theater and hall were removed to create the dining room. Taliesin is one mile north of Hillside; Midway Farm is about a half-mile north.

Exterior view of Hillside assembly hall (*Left*)

All aspects of the building provide views of the rich Wisconsin countryside that inspired so much of Wright's work.

E. Kaufmann Sr. House (Fallingwater)

Mill Run, Pennsylvania (1935)

Edgar J. Kaufmann Jr. had been an apprentice at Taliesin, and he brought his father and Wright together for the architect's first major commission in years: a rural retreat on the department store owner's wooded property in Mill Run, Pennsylvania. The Kaufmann family had vacationed there for years, enjoying the stream, Bear Run, with its waterfalls, and the beauty of the western Pennsylvania highlands. Fallingwater is the fullest realization of Wright's lifelong ideal of a living place completely at one with nature.

Constructed on three levels primarily of reinforced concrete, native sandstone, and glass, its soaring cantilevered balconies anchored in solid rock, the house appears to spring from the ledges of its wooded glen. Walls of glass form the south exposure, and a vertical shaft of mitered glass merges with stone and steel to overlook the stream.

The horizontal planes of the cantilevers are joined by rough sandstone walls of varying thickness laid in alternating courses. Most of the house's floor space is devoted to the stone-flagged living area, with its various activity spaces, and to the terraces that soar out in four directions. The other rooms take up only a small proportion of the house. The guest house, added in 1939, is reached by a winding covered walkway that makes optimum rhythmic use of curved and geometric concrete forms.

In 1963 Edgar Kaufmann Jr. presented Fallingwater to the Western Pennsylvania Conservancy, with some 1,500 acres of land. Long-term restoration and maintenance have been entrusted to the architectural firm of Wank Adams Slavin Associates. Fallingwater is one of seventeen structures designated by the American Institute of Architects to be retained as examples of Wright's architectural contribution to American culture. ▣ ▣ ▣

Concrete trellis over entrance driveway (Above)
This is one of several concrete trellises designed to filter natural light through hanging foliage. A bridge carries the driveway over Bear Run to the entrance.

Stairway to stream (Left)
A suspended stairway from the living room leads directly into Bear Run below, enhancing the sense of unity between house and waterfall.

E. KAUFMANN SR. HOUSE (FALLINGWATER)

In the years after its construction, Fallingwater would become one of the world's best-known private houses. People who knew nothing about architecture were just as captivated by it as the Kaufmann family and the experts, including other architects, who came to admire and expound.

In his book *Frank Lloyd Wright Drawings* (Harry N. Abrams, 1990), Bruce Brooks Pfeiffer of the Frank Lloyd Wright Foundation relates how the plan for the house germinated in Wright's mind for some time, from his first visit to the site with the Kaufmanns to the day he produced the design within a few hours. When Kaufmann came to Taliesin to view the plans, he was surprised to find that the house was placed directly above the cascade, rather than upstream, where one could see it. When asked why, Wright responded, "Not to look at your waterfall, but to live with it."

The large square living room on the main level has a suspended stairway leading directly down to the stream, and a cantilevered terrace at either end. The upper levels contain sleeping quarters opening onto stone-paved terraces with concrete trelliswork above. At one point, trees on the site pierce these canopies. The driveway crosses a bridge over the stream and leads to the main entry, which is flanked by a loggia. Many observers have pointed out that photographs cannot capture the full effect: the house must be viewed from all aspects, like a sculpture.

In 1938 Wright designed the guest house, above and behind the main building, reached by the covered walkway. This complex added substantially to the available space, comprising four additional bedrooms (three of them designated as servants' quarters), two baths, a lounge with fireplace, laundry room, four-car garage, and terrace. A pool was added later and the smaller bedrooms converted into offices after the house changed hands.

The rock ledges that form the landscape of the descending hillside are an integral part of the structure. Balconies and terraces ascend from the central core like the branches of a tree—a pattern from nature that took a vertical form in the triaxial Price Tower in Bartlesville, Oklahoma, some twenty years later.

Several Taliesin apprentices played a major role in the construction of Fallingwater: Robert Mosher supervised the early work, and Edgar Tafel completed the work from the second level upward. The Kaufmann family enjoyed the house for many years, and maintained a lifelong friendship with the architect.

**View of east facade,
from bridge** (Above)
*This Jacques Lipchitz sculpture is
suitably placed against the backdrop of
Fallingwater's rugged sandstone walls.*

Dressing room/study (Left)
*Edgar Kaufmann Sr.'s study is located
on the second level, directly above
the kitchen.*

South facade (Left)

A chamois color was chosen for the concrete elements of the house to harmonize with the sandstone and the natural setting. Native rhododendron and mountain laurel flourish on the site.

Living room, with fireplace (Right)

One of the four major boulders along the streambed was incorporated into the house as the living room hearth. The floors are of waxed flagstone.

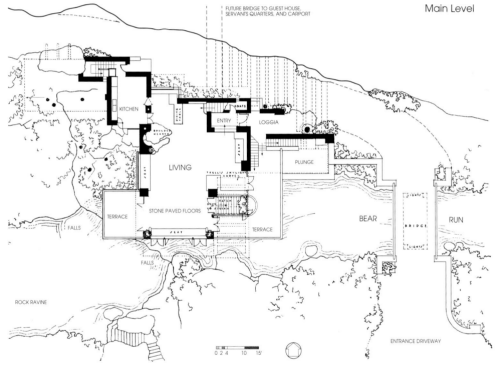

Main Level

Floor plan (Left)

At Fallingwater, a high proportion of the living space is outdoors, in the form of terraces, loggia, and plunge pool below the living room.

Living room, with east terrace in background (Below)

The living room comprises some 800 square feet of space, designed to be flexibly grouped for various activities by masonry piers, lighting, ceiling levels, and furniture arrangement. Simplicity, not grandeur, is the keynote.

View of west facade (Left, above)

The massive chimney core rises thirty feet from the site, serving as the trunk from which the cantilevered terraces branch out on all sides.

Living room, with entry in background (Left)

The living room is a study in restful buffs and grays, with window moldings and other accents in Cherokee red.

H. F. Johnson House (Wingspread)

Wind Point, Wisconsin (1937)

Wright called the great country house he designed for Herbert F. Johnson "the last Prairie house." In fact, it was one of the few that was actually built upon a prairie—Wind Point, a stretch of open country near Racine, Wisconsin. This was Wright's most expensive house, built for the client who had commissioned the Johnson Wax Building (1936), which would become a landmark in commercial architecture.

Wingspread forms a pinwheel extending from a massive brick chimney core with rounded ends, which contains five fireplaces on two levels. This is the focal point of the three-story living space, comprising entrance hall, dining area, library, music room, and mezzanine. The area is lighted from above by tiers of clerestory windows surrounding the masonry core. This central area, thirty feet high, is octagonal—Wright called it a wigwam—and the various spaces are defined by shallow steps and ceiling height.

The four wings of the house form different activity zones, as seen in the floor plan on the following page: children's quarters, master bedroom suite, guest bedrooms, and kitchen with servants' quarters. French doors open onto gardens, terraces, and the swimming pool on the south side of the house. Wright historian William Allin Storrer notes that the side walls of the pool were undercut so that they seem to disappear, leaving only water and reflection.

Sadly, Herbert Johnson was widowed before the house was completed in 1939. However, he lived in it for twenty years before making it the headquarters of the Johnson Foundation, which occupies it today. ▣   ▣   ▣

View of south facade (Left)

The pool is sheltered by two arms of the house, which is built primarily of red brick, pink Kasota sandstone, and cypress. The roofing material is red clay tile.

Clerestory of "wigwam" (Above)

The most striking feature of the interior is the thirty-foot-high curved chimney that ascends through the three-tier clerestory to the observatory outside.

Mezzanine level of "wigwam" (Below)

Golden oak veneer encloses this level, which has its own fireplace. The house is built on a square grid, which is incised into the red concrete floor.

View of north (bedroom) wing, with main entry (Above)

Wingspread was built on a former nature preserve, which provides unobstructed views of the Wisconsin prairie from every aspect of the level site.

North (bedroom) wing (Left)

The cantilevered master bedroom, clad in cypress, juts far from its brick supports, its thrust emphasized by the wood trellis above the balcony.

H. F. Johnson House (Wingspread)

Wingspread is one of the few Prairie houses that was not designed for a level suburban lot. Its twenty-acre Wind Point site had been part of a nature preserve, and the building is surrounded by evergreens, ponds, and deciduous trees. The house has 14,000 square feet of space and is constructed primarily of pink Kasota sandstone, Cherokee red brick, and cypress. The floors are of highly waxed red concrete incised into squares. A belvedere, or rooftop observation point, is reached by a dramatic spiral stairway that repeats the curvilinear form of the huge chimney, with its deeply raked mortar joints.

The principal ornamentation is the craftsmanship of Wingspread's materials, from warm expanses of oak veneer to the distinctive masses of brick and sandstone. The furniture, much of it built-in, is simple and comfortable, arranged around the various hearths and grouped outdoors to invite contemplation of the pool and landscape. Wood sun decks, French doors, rectangular windows, and skylights illuminate the scene. Essentially, the house remains as it was built, apart from conversion of several carports on the west side into office space for the Johnson Foundation.

In the north wing, the master bedroom extends far from the masonry foundation on a wood-and-steel cantilever clad in wood siding. A pierced canopy (trellis) projects over the balcony, contributing to the overall effect of a structure floating above the landscape.

The rooftop observatory, enclosed in curved glass, continues the rhythmic flow of the masonry core and the veneered planes of the curving balcony. These lines are reprised in the barrel chairs, originally designed for the Darwin D. Martin house in Buffalo, New York (1904), and also used at Taliesin. A few carefully selected works of art complement both house and grounds.

In the series of four lectures that Wright delivered in London at the invitation of the Royal Institute of British Architects, he described Wingspread as having "something of the clean-limbed sense of power adapted to purpose which you find in a well-poised plane or ocean liner." He added that "this is no mere aesthetic, it is constitutional, I assure you. This is probably one of the most complete, best constructed and most expensive houses it has ever been my good fortune to build."

JR

S HERBERT F JOHNSON

RACINE WISCONSIN

WRIGHT ARCHITECT

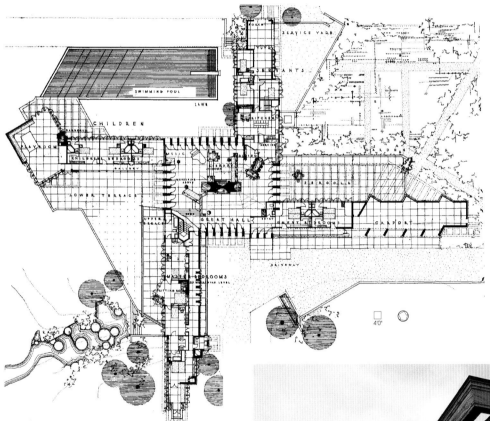

Floor plan (Above)

As the plan suggests, Wingspread was
the largest and most expensive
residential commission Wright had
carried out to that date. All its
materials were the finest available.

A   COUNTRY   D W

TALIESIN WEST

SCOTTSDALE, ARIZONA (1937)

This desert retreat had its prototype in Ocatillo Camp, where Wright and seven draftsmen spent the winter of 1928–29 working on plans for the proposed resort hotel San Marcos in the Desert at Chandler, Arizona. The previous year, Wright had designed the greater part of the Arizona Biltmore Hotel in Phoenix as consultant to the architect Albert Chase McArthur. Both these forays provided welcome relief from the bitter winters of Wisconsin, which were especially trying because Taliesin had no central heating system. Ocatillo Camp was a modest complex of board and canvas on wood frames built entirely by hand, but Taliesin West would become another landmark in contemporary architecture.

The triangular theme derives from the mountains surrounding the site, on a mesa near Scottsdale. From 1937 onward, members of the Taliesin Fellowship worked on the permanent camp during the winter months. Continuously enlarged and revised, its basic form remained constant: massive base walls of desert rubblestone embedded in concrete, surmounted by redwood frames and expanses of white canvas, like a sailing ship. The diffused light softened the harsh glare of the sun and provided an ideal environment for both studio and living quarters. The long straight axis is slashed by diagonal framing, and the stark forms of desert plants like the saguaro cactus are incorporated into the structure.

Multicolored stone from the site edges the triangular pool, with a fountain that brings the soothing sound of water to the arid surroundings. Taliesin West is one of seventeen structures designated by the American Institute of Architects to be retained as examples of Wright's architectural contribution to American culture. ▣   ▣   ▣

Pergola (Above)
The pergola extends the full length of the drafting studio, throwing a pattern of shadows on the ground below it.

Bell tower, with partial view of loggia to the left (Left, above)
Spiky desert plants are the foreground to the tower's stark forms, which recall the masonry of the original Southwestern builders, the Pueblo peoples.

Terraced gardens (Above)
Like a Japanese garden, this one uses stone as others do plant materials to form a rhythmic, balanced design.

Exterior of drafting studio
(Right)
Composed of basalt stone, the angular stone walls of Taliesin West with their asymmetrical movement adeptly reflect the desert's dynamic structures and textures.

TALIESIN WEST

Like its Wisconsin counterpart, the Scottsdale home and studio is essentially a series of buildings linked by partially covered walkways, terraces, and courtyards. Broad, shallow steps contrast with the buildings' vertical rooflines and standing stones, and the angular profiles of the nearby mountains. With characteristic enthusiasm, Wright described the Fellowship's early years at Taliesin West in his 1943 autobiography:

"For the designing of our buildings, certain forms already abounded…tremendous drifts and heaps of sun-burned desert rocks were nearby to be used. From first to last, thousands of cords of stone, carloads of cement, carloads of redwood, acres of stout white canvas doubled over wood frames four feet by eight feet…. We devised a light canvas covered redwood framework resting upon this massive stone masonry that belonged to the mountain slopes all around. On a fair day, when these white tops and side flaps were flung open, the desert air and the birds flew clear through."

As most of the desert stones had one flat side, this face was left exposed when the concrete was poured into the forms. Surplus mortar was chipped away from the edges, and the stones were often washed with acid to bring out their colors, including mauve, orange, yellow, and reddish brown. The first structure, built as living quarters for the Wrights, was called Sun Trap, eventually remodeled into Sun Cottage. As in all of Wright's residences, the hearth remains the focal point of the dwelling. Additions included a fourth bedroom and a separate cottage near the front entrance.

Over time, the interior became richly embellished with gold pile carpeting, woven textiles, Native American pottery—even a grand piano. Wright's private office, the drafting room, and the garden room were originally covered by canvas, but from 1945 glass was increasingly used, along with synthetic materials like plastic and fiberglass that maintained the translucent quality of the light. The Wright family and the Fellowship gathered in the garden room to entertain guests and enjoy musical concerts.

After World War II, the Cabaret Theatre was added north of the drafting room to accommodate growing numbers of guests and their entertainment. When this was outgrown, in the early 1950s, the Music Pavilion was added as a right-angle attachment. The pavilion has its own terrace and foyer. The large drafting room serves the needs of the Fellowship, and the staff of the Frank Lloyd Wright Memorial Foundation has its permanent quarters on the site. The entrance is marked by the stone lighting tower with its sculptural sign, an expression of Wright's "square within a square" in Cherokee red.

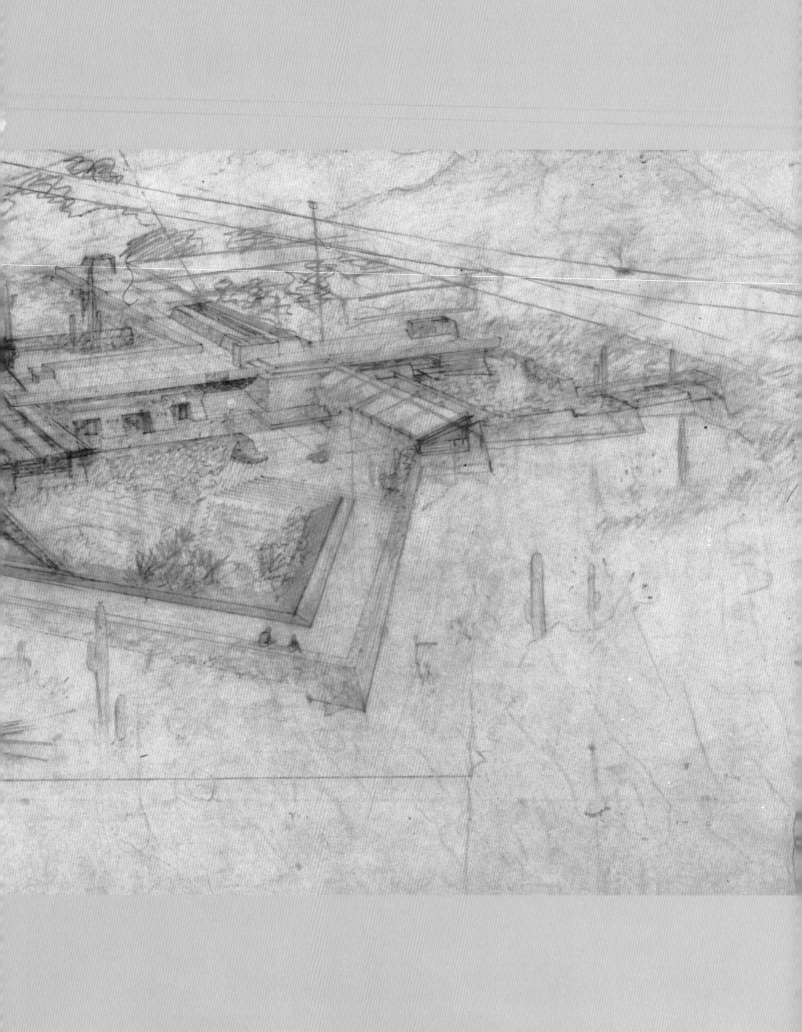

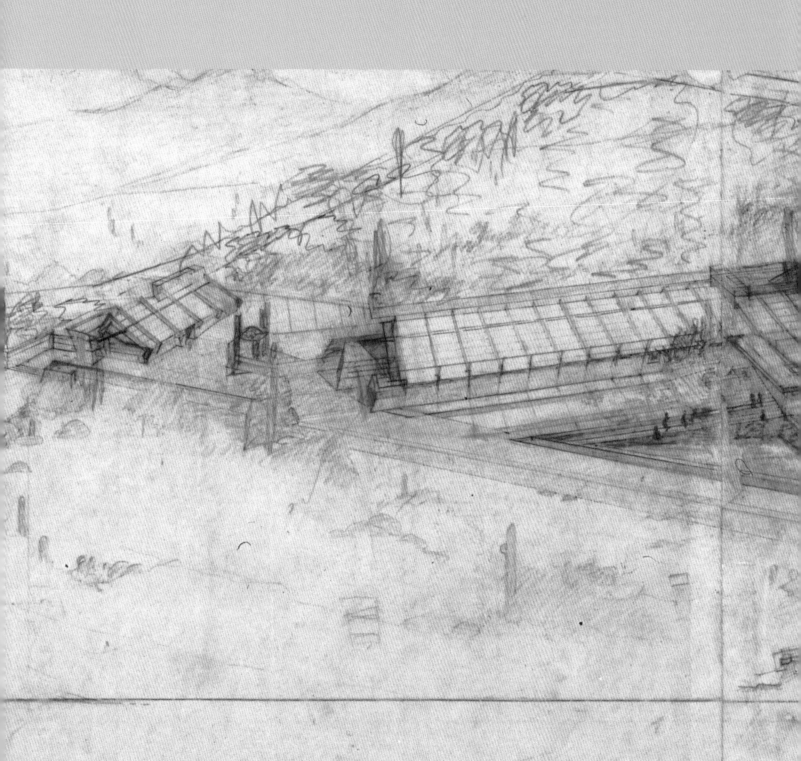

View of Taliesin West, with landscape (Right)
Despite the differences in climate and topography, Taliesin West has many features in common with Taliesin I. Both are actually many separate buildings connected by walkways, courts, and terraces and surrounded by natural vegetation.

View of loggia (Left)
Native vegetation softens the angular rubblestone walls and piers of this dramatic facade, which draws inspiration from the jagged peaks surrounding Maricopa Mesa.

Lighting pylon, with fountains and sculptural sign (Above)
The welcome sight and sound of running water surround the rugged lighting pylon with its sign derived from Wright's favorite emblem, the "square within a square."

Drafting studio (Above)
Triangular redwood forms dominate the drafting studio, which has been in continuous use since its construction in 1937 by the Taliesin Fellowship. The Arizona desert was a welcome refuge from the freezing Wisconsin winters at Taliesin I.

Fireplace in Wright's sitting room (Left)
Wright's private quarters were among the original living spaces on the site of Taliesin West. The stone foundation is in strong contrast with the redwood-and-canvas superstructure. Eventually, the canvas was replaced by synthetic materials.

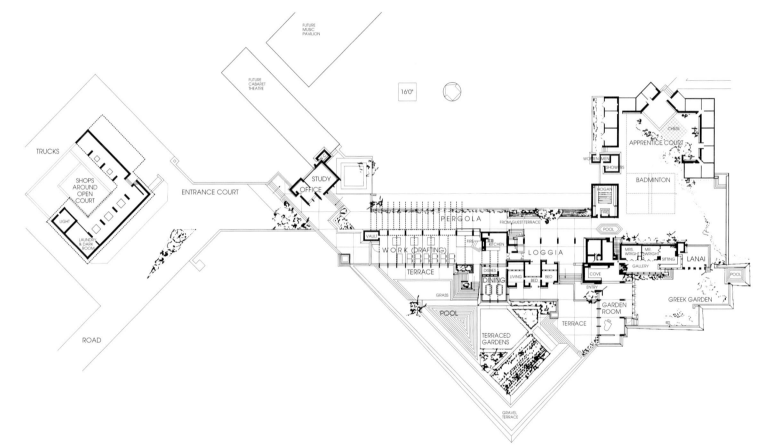

Floor plan (*Above*)
General plan of Taliesin West in its earliest years: The growth of the Fellowship after World War II led to many additions and remodelings of this original plan.

View of south facade, with pool (*Left*)
The triangular pool restates the major geometric theme of the complex, offering the contrast of an oasis to the desert's aridity.

Annie Merner Pfeiffer Chapel

Florida Southern College, Lakeland, Florida (1938)

The skylighted bell tower of the hexagonal Pfeiffer Chapel is the most vertical feature on the Florida Southern College campus, for which Wright drew a master plan in 1938. Ludd Spivey, president of the Methodist liberal arts college, had enlisted his help in designing a "college of tomorrow," and Wright's lifelong interest in progressive education was engaged immediately. The Pfeiffer Chapel was the first of twelve integrated structures built for the college over a twenty-year period.

The plan was kept to a low scale congruent with the flat site, which is bordered by citrus orchards and faces a lake. Primary building materials for the chapel and other structures were reinforced cast concrete and sand-cast concrete blocks containing limestone from local shells and corals. Many of the blocks are inset with colored glass that refracts the sunlight. Wright called the campus "Child of the Sun."

The chapel bell tower has embossed rectangular patterns on either side of a central concrete panel. It rises into a breezeway-shaped skylight supported by triangular steel beams. The design called for hanging plants in concrete planters to filter the light to the interior, which is reminiscent of the Unity Temple sanctuary in its correlation of pulpit, choir, and congregation. Until recently, up to eight hundred students could be seated in diagonal rows facing the triangular stage for the pulpit. The stage area has now been enlarged and the chapel's capacity reduced by installation of new seating. The choir occupies a balcony above the stage, screened by a lattice of patterned concrete block. A continuous covered esplanade connects the chapel and all the other Wright-designed buildings on the campus, which now includes several buildings by other architects. ▣ ▣ ▣

Stairwell (Below)

The intimacy of the stairwells makes the colored, L-shaped glass in the sand-cast blocks particularly effective.

View of north facade (Left)

The first part of the campus to be constructed after the master plan was conceived in 1938, the esplanade runs the entire length of the chapel on the north side.

View of chapel pulpit (Above)

The soaring skylighted bell tower casts shadows across the triangular stage area, from which the pulpit faces the congregation.

Annie Merner Pfeiffer Chapel

Wright's sensitivity to the demands of topography and climate was a major element in his design for the Pfeiffer Chapel and the other buildings at Florida Southern College. The location, forty miles inland from the Gulf of Mexico near Tampa, suggested such features as low, light-colored buildings to reduce interior heat and a decorative concrete esplanade to ward off tropical rainstorms and serve as a breezeway. This latter feature is common to Gulf Coast vernacular architecture. As early as 1890, Wright had designed a vacation bungalow for his employer and mentor Louis Sullivan in Ocean Springs, Mississippi, facing Davis Bayou on the Gulf. It has a full-width veranda along the front and both sides of the T-shaped plan.

by Wright's Unitarian backgound and characterizes most of his ecclesiastical architecture, which is largely free of nonintegral ornament and images. Instead, the interior fosters a sense of unity and repose.

Originally, the chapel had full-length doors to balconies on either side, but these were replaced by casement windows with air-conditioning ducts at sill level. The sand-cast concrete block of the tower is inset with colored, L-shaped glass that creates a sense of delicacy vis-à-vis the concrete. The carillon, an electronic bell system, had to be removed from the tower, because the space was so resonant that Lakeland residents complained about the noise. The hanging plants that filtered the daylight from above also posed problems, for structural reasons.

Another consideration was Wright's rejection of the conventional American campus, derived largely from Gothic, Federalist, and Neoclassic prototypes. He felt that young people in a democratic society should have an educational environment suited to their needs and culture, rather than one based on outmoded European models. Thus, he was closely attuned to Dr. Spivey's request for a "college of tomorrow": The campus is devoid of stone towers, ivy, and quadrangles.

The Pfeiffer Chapel continues the experiments of the 1930s in concrete cantilevers and incorporates the concrete-block experience gained during the 1920s. The overall plan is hexagonal, designed on a grid of six-foot-square design units as noted at bottom right on the floor plan. The spare yet expansive worship space is informed

In *Frank Lloyd Wright and the Meaning of Materials* (Van Nostrand Reinhold, 1994), Terry L. Patterson observes that "the perforated concrete choir screen in the Pfeiffer Chapel is among the most plastic of Wright's noncurvilinear patterned concrete. The complex outline of each hole, although consisting of straight lines, seems almost curvilinear.... Unlike a solid plane that is distinguished from a mass only at its edges, the openings in the screen frequently reveal the concrete's thickness, which verifies the construction as being a slab like form." In the Pfeiffer Chapel, patterned cast concrete and decorative concrete block are often indistinguishable. This feature carries over to the triangular piers of the esplanade, which have a rectangular pattern on the upper blocks that recurs as notching along the edge of the flat, cast-concrete canopy.

Chapel interior (Left)
Ceiling levels at various heights help define the hexagonal form of the chapel, which has minimal ornamentation apart from perforated screens of wood and concrete.

View of west facade (Right)
Concrete cantilevers figure prominently in the composition of the chapel, the skylighted bell tower of which overlooks the rest of the campus.

Esplanade (Left)
Sand-cast concrete blocks form the supports for the broad eaves of this esplanade, which connects all of Wright's buildings on the Florida Southern College campus.

Chapel interior, facing northwest (Below)
Many of the walls of the chapel were built with sand-cast blocks decorated with colored, L-shaped glass.

Esplanade (Above)
The geometric forms of the esplanade not only strike a unifying note on the campus, but afford protection from Florida's tropical sun and brief torrential rainstorms.

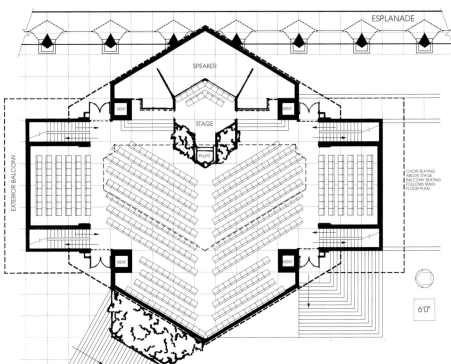

Floor plan *(Right)*

The pulpit projects from the triangular stage area toward the diagonal seating area for the congregation. Recent remodeling has reduced the original seating capacity of eight hundred to around five hundred.

ESPLANADE

SPEAKER

VENT

STAGE

VENT

EXTERIOR BALCONY

PULPIT

CHOIR SEATING
ABOVE STAGE.
BALCONY SEATING
FOLLOWS MAIN
FLOOR PLAN.

VENT

VENT

6'0"

Beth Sholom Synagogue

Elkins Park, Pennsylvania (1954)

The rendering illustrates the power expressed in the house of worship commissioned by the congregation of Beth Sholom, under the leadership of Rabbi Mortimer J. Cohen. It was one of Wright's most significant achievements. Rabbi Cohen worked closely with the architect from the building's inception, and Wright's imagination was captured by the rabbi's desire that the temple should be "a mountain of light." Wright's response was a great tapering structure of aluminum, steel, glass, and fiberglass that rose from an approximately hexagonal base on a tripod formed by steel and concrete uprights. Its inspiration is Mount Sinai, in the Egyptian desert, where the Jewish people received the Torah, a symbol of light housed in the ark of every synagogue.

Each of Beth Sholom's three exterior ridges bears abstract representations of the menorah, another sign of light inseparable from Jewish history and belief. The menorah recurs in the main-level temple and the chapel, or Sisterhood Sanctuary, on the lower level, which has its own ark and seats 250 people. The main sanctuary seats more than 1,000, and the great space is unobstructed by supporting beams because it is suspended from the building's 160-ton tripod frame.

The design was derived in part from Wright's unbuilt Steel Cathedral of 1925–26, a visionary project for housing churches and temples of different denominations under one massive superstructure of steel and glass. The central portion was to rise over a huge space called the Hall of the Elements, into which light would pour from above to illuminate the various worship spaces and a great courtyard. He described the plan as "the devotional church of churches."

Beth Sholom is one of seventeen structures designated by the American Institute of Architects to be retained as examples of Wright's architectural contribution to American culture. ⊡ ⊡ ⊡

Main sanctuary, with ark *(Right)*
Two of the most striking features of this worship space are the beautiful ark for the Torah, designed in collaboration with Rabbi Cohen, and the triangular stained-glass chandelier symbolizing both light and the inexpressible attributes of the Divine.

Perspective view of west facade *(Left)*
This view illustrates how the triangular elements of the concrete base are reprised in the equilateral triangle of the translucent, tentlike superstructure.

South facade at night *(Below)*
Many critics believe that Beth Sholom is the apex of Wright's achievement in ecclesiastical architecture.

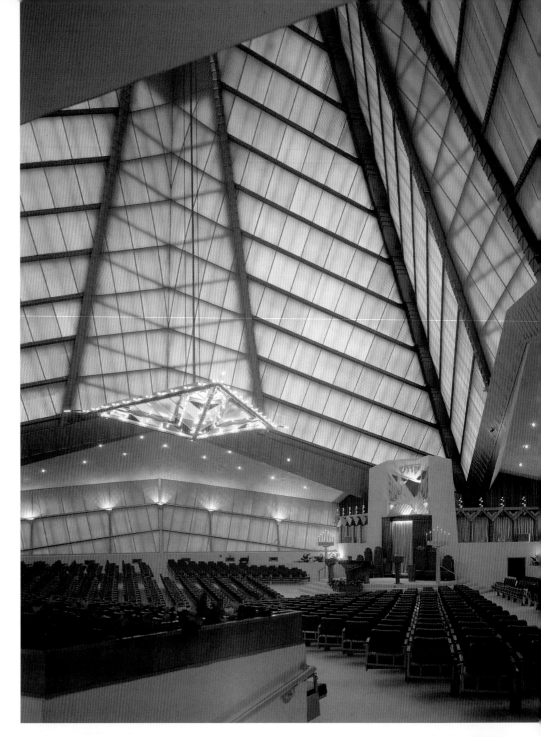

The Sisterhood Sanctuary *(Right)*
Located below the temple area, this chapel seats 250 women and has its own ark.

B eth Sholom was the antithesis of what Wright had called "starched churches." In a scathing book review of *The Church Beautiful*, published in the *Christian Register* in 1946, he asked: "Cannot religion be brought into a human scale? Can it not be humanized and natural? Must 'church architecture' be starched stiff as a hard collar and the symbols of worship be no more inspiring than a black bow tie or a pair of suspenders?" Elsewhere in the same review, he stated that the church of the future had yet to be built. A decade later, he had undertaken to build it.

The unique quality of the temple's natural lighting results from a two-part layer of translucent panels with airspace between for insulation. The exterior wall/roof material is blasted white corrugated wire glass; the interior, cream-colored corrugated fiberglass. Aluminum cover strips bind the outer and inner layers. At night, the entire structure glows with interior artificial light.

A ground-level vestibule leads down toward the chapel and common areas, one of which is connected by a sheltered walkway to the adjacent school. The main auditorium is reached by shallow, curving flights of stairs to the left and right of the entrance. The interior space slopes down gently toward the ark, faced by congregational seating set in blocks at various levels. The woodwork is oiled walnut stained in shades of brown and tan.

The lower level, accessed by a set of stairs from the vestibule, has ample space for the congregation's social activities: two large lounges and a kitchen, smaller men's and women's lounges with adjacent bathrooms, and, behind the chapel dais, storage and utility areas. The cantor's and rabbi's studies are on the temple level, behind the ark.

The multicolored glass chandelier suspended over the temple area was designed to express aspects of the Divine, as defined in the mystical kabbala, since graphic representations of God are forbidden by Jewish law and custom. This prohibition dates back to the revelation on Mount Sinai, when "graven images" were associated with the polytheistic beliefs of neighboring peoples. The triangular canopy that projects over the entrance represents hands joined in benediction over the congregation. Rabbi Cohen worked so closely with Wright on the integration of Jewish symbolism into the structure that he is credited on the plans as codesigner. The two became good friends in the course of working on the project, which many consider Wright's most expressive house of worship. Haskell Culwell was the general contractor for the building. Beth Sholom appears in an unpublished drawing for Wright's book *The Living City* (Horizon Press, 1958). Wright died only five months before the temple was dedicated.

Beth Sholom Synagogue can be perceived as part of Wright's spiritual legacy, imbued with Wright's Unitarian and transcendentalist heritage. As he said in the last years of his life: "All the more because I study Nature do I revere God, because Nature is all the body of God we will ever know."

Scheme II   American Symposia for Battle Creek... Santa Cat...
Things increased up to 10000 watts
on Luminished to 500.
Various forms by Modification of power — infinite

Menorah, detail (Above)
Abstractions of the seven-branched menorah project from all three ridges of the synagogue's steel-tripod framework.

West facade at night (Far left)
Wright's imagination was fired by Rabbi Cohen's vision of the temple as "a mountain of light," like Mount Sinai. Here, Jewish symbolism and its architectural expression are fully realized.

Main sanctuary, with upper vestibule in background (Above)
The upper vestibule, with memorial tablets at either end, gives access to the sanctuary—a large space unobstructed by supporting members.

Vestibule (Left)
At the main entrance, the vestibule gives access by stairs to both the main sanctuary and the lower level, with its chapel, lounges, and kitchen facilities.

Entrance (Right)
The triangular canopy over the main entrance, symbolizing hands joined in benediction over the congregation, reprises the main geometric theme of the structure.

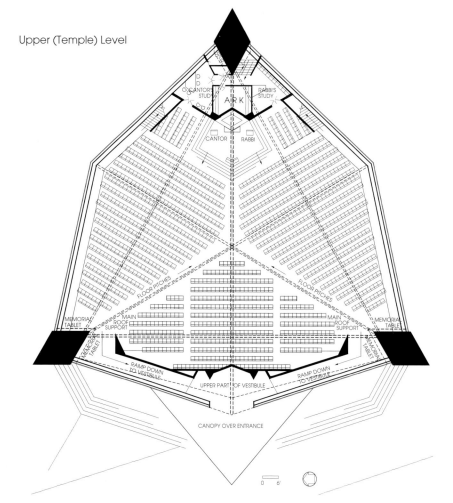

Upper (Temple) Level

Floor plan (Right)
This complex plan of the upper
(temple) level shows both the
hexagonal concrete base of the
structure and the supporting members
that carry walls and roof to the apex.

5420.01

ANNUNCIATION GREEK ORTHODOX CHURCH

WAUWATOSA, WISCONSIN (1956)

The rendering for Wright's last ecclesiastical commission, carried out for Milwaukee's Greek Orthodox community, shows how two symbols primary to that faith—the arch and the cross—are combined in a simple, elegant form. Wright's third wife, Olgivanna, a native of Montenegro, had grown up in the Greek Orthodox faith, and she helped to clarify his focus on its tradition, as Rabbi Cohen had done for the Judaic background of Beth Sholom.

The ground plan is a Greek cross (i.e., having arms of equal length). The upper part of the building is carried on concrete piers that support the bowl-shaped balcony covered by the dome of the roof. The main entrance, at ground level, is a broad archway reached by wide, shallow stone steps. The arch is repeated in the windows that encircle the balcony, and in the precast sun screen that projects over the top level.

Wright's understanding of Byzantine architecture is also apparent in this contemporary interpretation: "The arch was Byzantine," he wrote, "and is a sophisticated building act resulting in more sophisticated forms than the lintel of the Mayan, Egyptian, or Greek. Yet it is essentially primitive masonry. Byzantine architecture lived anew by the arch. The arch sprung from the caps of stone posts and found its way into roofing by way of the low, heavy stone dome.... The Byzantine sense of form seems neither East nor West but belongs to both."

As the floor plan (overleaf) indicates, the Greek cross inscribed in a circle creates the worship space (designated "auditorium"). Natural overhead light is provided by a ring of glass spheres below the shallow dome. The primary construction materials are cast concrete, steel, aluminum, and glass. ▣   ▣   ▣

Front facade (Left)

The impressive configuration of cross and dome forms a balanced whole reflected in the pool before the church.

Trellis awning (Right)

At the roofline, the ornamental aluminum brackets with sharp, lancelike points project from the face of the church just below the precast sunscreen.

Balcony level and ceiling (Below)

The curving lines of the balcony follow the circular theme of the structure and its Byzantine domed ceiling.

Annunciation Greek Orthodox Church

odern engineering made it possible for Wright to execute this plan for a church that is "neither East nor West but belongs to both." Some of the technical challenges involved are explained by William Allin Storrer in *The Frank Lloyd Wright Companion* (University of Chicago Press, 1993):

"The roof structure is a concrete shell dome originally surfaced in blue ceramic mosaic tile and, to withstand extreme temperature changes, supported on thousands of ball bearings. The roof dome, then, rides on these ball bearings set in steel rails, supported by reinforced-concrete cylindrical trussing…. In turn, the truss is held aloft by four concrete piers."

Unfortunately, the roof tiles soon heaved with the frost, causing damage to the interior ceiling; they were replaced with a synthetic plastic resin.

The primary interior color is gold, illuminating the ceiling, carpeting, and delicate metalwork (of gold-anodized aluminum developed by the Alcoa Corporation). Decorative circles and semicircles occur throughout the metalwork, including the top of the icon screen before the altar. There, a diamond motif across the screen complements the rich colors of the images and contributes to the symbolic effect of a crown, representing Christ triumphant, a major theme in Byzantine iconography. The images of the saints are elegant and attenuated in the Byzantine manner.

The circular theme is repeated in the flight of steps to the main entrance, which is framed by a convex arch. Massive piers flanking the steps carry pedestal urns that echo the disklike shape of the upper level. The *narthex*, or lobby, opens into the main worship space, while the lower level is accessed by several stairways. Social and educational activities are carried out on the lower level, which has a circular banquet hall with stage, kitchen, choir robing room, offices, chapel, and Sunday school classrooms.

This church is one of Wright's last major concrete buildings, along with the Marin County Civic Center and the Guggenheim Museum in New York City (following page). In all three, concrete was used with the high degree of plasticity that marked his later work. In *The Seven Ages of Frank Lloyd Wright: A New Appraisal* (Capra Press, 1993), architect Donald W. Hoppen, who came from England to study with Wright at Taliesin, traces the evolution of his design forms, from the rectangular planes of the early Prairie period through the circular and spiral designs of his last years. Hoppen believes that Wright achieved "a new dimension of spatial energy" in the convex forms of the Greek Orthodox church.

Wright's reverence for Byzantine architecture was powerfully expressed in the book he cowrote with Baker Brownell, *Architecture and Modern Life* (Harper & Brothers, 1937). There he stated that, "The Byzantine building was more nobly stone than any Gothic architecture. It was no less truly stone than…Mayan architecture. Into Byzantine buildings went the riches of the East in metals, weaving images and ritual…. A robust spirit lived in Byzantine work. It still grappled earth forcefully with simple purpose and complete individuality." It was the spirit of Byzantium that informed Annunciation.

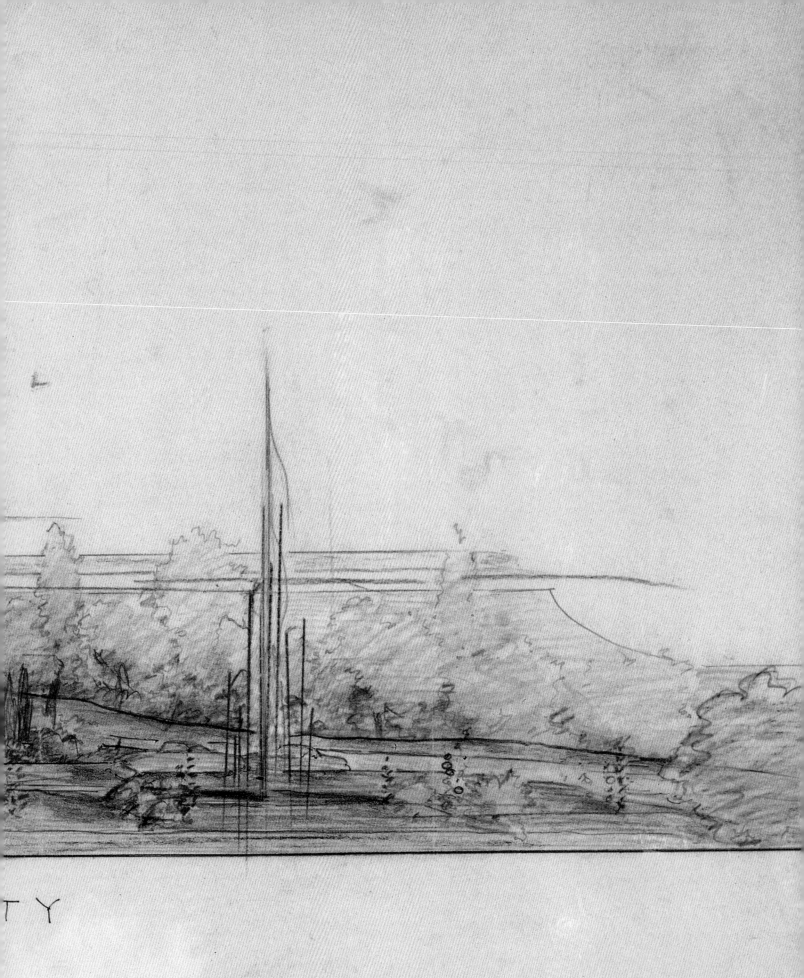

TY

KEE HELLENIC COMMUNI

ARCHITECT

Main entrance (Far left)
The convex shape of the main entrance is a variation on the arch, one of the two primary symbols in the Greek Orthodox faith.

Greek-cross sculpture at approach to church (Left)
The equal-armed Greek cross is inscribed in a circle in this concrete sculpture marking the approach to the Hellenistic house of worship.

View of sanctuary, with icon screen (Below)
The focal point of this graceful sanctuary is the altar, with its delicate icon screen crowned with light.

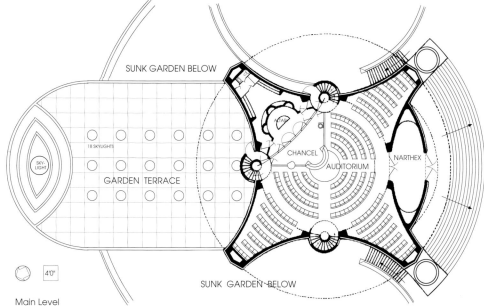

SUNK GARDEN BELOW

18 SKYLIGHTS

SKY-LIGHT

GARDEN TERRACE

STAIR

CHANCEL

AUDITORIUM

NARTHEX

SUNK GARDEN BELOW

4'0"

Main Level

Priest and congregation (Below)
Many longtime members of Milwaukee's tight-knit Greek Orthodox community were closely involved in the planning and financing of Annunciation.

Floor plan (Above)
Congregational seating occupies three of the four arms of the cruciform base, with the chancel in the fourth arm. A large terrace adjoins the building.

CHURCH FOR THE MILWA

MILWAUKEE, WISCONSIN

FRANK LLOYD WRIGHT,

Solomon R. Guggenheim Museum

New York, New York (1956)

Hundreds of conceptual sketches, studies, and developmental drawings were executed on the arduous path from the Guggenheim Museum's original design in 1943 to its construction in the late 1950s—sixteen years of revisions, delays, and disappointments in the latter part of Wright's long career. Before it was over, he had to take an apartment in New York's Plaza Hotel to deal with the ceaseless demands of the project.

The commission came from the wealthy collector of non-objective art Solomon R. Guggenheim, who asked Wright for a museum unlike any other. Curator Hilla Rebay was a moving force behind the project. The many delays in implementing the plan included the building moratorium imposed by World War II and the difficulty of finding a suitable site in expensive Manhattan.

The spiral form that figured in the design from the earliest stage went through several versions: with tiers of the same size, or growing progressively smaller toward the top, or expanding in size as the building rose. The latter choice—that of the expanding spiral—made the best use of the available site, while combining structural and spatial principles toward which Wright had worked throughout his career.

The primary construction material is concrete, both sprayed and poured into forms. Inside the building, a shallow spiraling ramp follows the curvilinear form of the exterior. Wright intended it to conduct the visitors from the topmost tier, reached by elevator, to the bottom of the ramp, viewing the artworks along the way.

The Guggenheim Museum is one of seventeen structures designated by the American Institute of Architects to be retained as examples of Wright's architectural contribution to American culture. ▣ ▣ ▣

Atrium skylight (Left)

The imposing skylight-dome enhances proper viewing of the artwork with unusually abundant natural lighting. Wright's skillful engineering solved lighting problems that had always plagued conventional museums.

View of entry ramp (Right)

From every level, one can view the central court below with its shallow pool. The court is often used for receptions and other large gatherings.

Galleries, with artwork (Above)

Patrons of the museum may view its special exhibitions by descending the spiral ramp of the main gallery.

View of main entrance (Right)

Lettering for the incised brass signs was designed by John Ottenheimer. Originally, the museum was to be called the Museum of Non-Objective Painting. The name was changed after Mr. Guggenheim's death in 1949, six years after Wright received the commission.

THE SOLOMON R GUG

The unconventional design for the building was one of the factors that delayed its construction. Artists feared that its unusual shape and the pitch of the ramp would make it impossible to exhibit their works. Similar concerns were expressed by the museum's board of trustees and its first director, James Johnson Sweeney. Curator Rebay objected to the design on grounds that the building might overpower the works of art. While the museum was under construction, Wright prepared a series of interior perspectives, with replications of specific paintings in the collection, to show how the exhibitions would be mounted.

Attached to "the Ziggurat," as Wright called the main building, is a small office wing, identified on the floor plan as the "Monitor." Taliesin architect William Wesley Peters worked on the design with Mendel Glickman. William Short supervised construction with David Wheatley and Morton Deison.

As early as 1946, Wright prepared an article for the *Magazine of Art* explaining his concept of the building. It says in part:

"An interesting feature of the building is the fact that grandomania is discarded. All in all, it is proportioned to the scale of the human figure. This is true not only in every detail of the new gallery but of the organization and uses of the building itself as a whole.... the paintings it displays will be at home in an environment admirably adapted to their character. The entire structure will be securely founded upon bedrock fifty feet below the street level and will be of the most enduring character known to modern science. Requiring little or no maintenance, the edifice is virtually indestructible by natural forces—earthquake-proof, fireproof, and storm-proof."

Published with this article, which also appeared in *The Architectural Forum* (January 1946), was a cutaway model of the proposed museum showing its innovative use of the spiral ramp, peripheral skylight, and central court. Solomon R. Guggenheim had already countersigned the working drawings to indicate his approval. However, New York City parks commissioner Robert Moses remained unconvinced. A cousin of Wright's by marriage and a personal friend, he steadily opposed the museum's design and even the non-objective paintings that it would house. In fact, the two were wholly opposed on the subject of city planning. Their vigorous disputes were published in *The New York Times* and filled reams of personal correspondence over a ten-year period, until a building permit was issued at last in 1956. Even then, controversy swirled around the structure both before and after its opening.

During the 1980s, New York City planners approved an addition to the structure, which was given status by the Historic Buildings and Landmarks Commission shortly after the addition was begun. The marble veneer Wright had chosen to finish the exterior was never applied, due to its high cost. Alterations to the building include a second-level gallery created from office space to house the Justin K. Thannhauser collection, acquired after Wright's death. The original driveway was filled in with a bookstore and cafe. As William Allin Storrer reports in *The Frank Lloyd Wright Companion* (University of Chicago Press, 1993): "The bookstore remains even after the so-called restoration. The main gallery skylights were covered, destroying Wright's lighting effects. In 1992 the main gallery was restored to Wright's intended design."

Main gallery (Far left)
The concept of a central shaft of space lighted from above can be traced in Wright's work, from the Larkin Building and Unity Temple in the early 1900s to this revolutionary art museum in Manhattan of the late 1950s.

Ground level of main gallery (Below)
When the museum opened on upper Fifth Avenue in 1959, it was both praised and vilified by critics and public alike. Even now, it is a controversial building. Wright told his apprentices that he had finally designed it to please himself.

View of facade, facing Fifth Avenue (Left)

In the Guggenheim Museum, Wright took his experiments in the plasticity of concrete forms to the limit. The design underwent countless revisions from its inception in 1943 to construction a decade and a half later.

Ground Level

8'0"

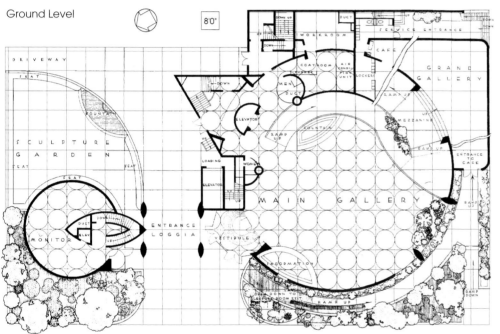

Floor plan (Above)

Plan of ground level: The main gallery, with its attendant office and storage space, is flanked by a small office wing called the "Monitor," with a pool and sculpture garden.

View across the galleries (Right)

The museum's spiraling ramp is three quarters of a mile long and has a grade of 3 percent. It was designed so that visitors could trace the unfolding of an artist's career as they move down the ramp, from the elevator near the top to the ground level.

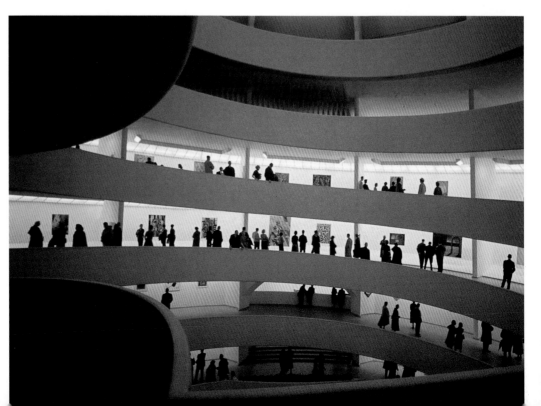

MARIN COUNTY CIVIC CENTER

ʃAN RAFAEL, CALIFORNIA (1957)

The Marin County Civic Center was designed two years before Wright's death and completed afterward by Taliesin Architects Ltd. and Aaron Green. At the top left of the perspective is the nearly circular post office, a free-standing structure of concrete block and forms completed in 1962. This was Wright's only building for the federal government. County offices and courts occupy the wings extending from the domed library to the adjacent hills. These wings are actually two buildings in parallel. The Administration Building, at left, was completed in 1962, the Hall of Justice in 1970. The two structures at the far right of the drawing were never built: the tentlike pavilion for state and county fairs and the amphitheater at the lower right of the lagoon.

The multilevel arcaded buildings span the shallow valleys between the hillsides on the site; the driveway passes through a concrete arcade under each wing. The concrete pylon with aluminum cladding, which rises from a prowlike terrace where the buildings join, was designed to serve as a ventilation tower and radio antenna.

The concrete barrel-vaulted rooflines cover double rows of offices lining a central well capped by plastic skylights tinted blue (Wright had specified a gold tone, but the manufacturer could not guarantee it). The plexiglass-covered court between the two buildings has plantings that can be viewed from the galleries at every level, as in the Guggenheim Museum.

Aaron Green, working from his ʃan Francisco office, designed the circular courtrooms for the Hall of Justice, which has movable walls and partitions to accommodate the changing needs of the county government. The third (topmost) level of the Administration Building houses educational services and the county library. The roofs of the complex, with their precast designs, are of concrete coated with polymer paint. ▣ ▣ ▣

View of west facade *(Left)*
The library dome acts as a visual "hinge" that joins the two buildings, which were completed separately in 1962 and 1970.

View of Civic Center before construction of Hall of Justice *(Below)*
The commanding pylon near the dome marks one end of the Administration Building (the first half of the project, completed three years after Wright's death).

Pylon and north end of Administration Building *(Above)*
Designed as a ventilation shaft and radio antenna, the pylon, like the roofline, has ornamental metal cladding.

Hall of Justice *(Below)*
The multilevel arcades of the Hall of Justice, completed in 1970, have a rhythmic quality which suggests the notes of a musical composition.

The civic center's main buildings appear to have concrete facades. In fact, only the base is cast-in-place concrete; the walls above are stucco with steel framing. The arcades become progressively smaller as the buildings rise; the smallest arches, at the topmost level, form complete circles. Glass walls run nearly the length of each floor, recessed behind the arcades. Grilles of steel pipe painted terra-cotta red cover the larger windows, contrasting with the sand-colored walls. Metal recurs in decorative elements throughout the complex, including aluminum gates formed of bent piping, and anodized aluminum trim on the triangular tower. Metal spheres are attached to the lower edges of the overhanging roofs. The plasticity of the concrete elements here is reminiscent of several other works of this period, including the Annunciation Greek Orthodox Church at Wauwatosa, Wisconsin, and New York City's Guggenheim Museum (both 1956).

Many features of the civic center were forecast in the twelve-foot-square model of Broadacre City, built by Wright and members of the Taliesin Fellowship in 1934 to illustrate his ideas on urban planning appropriate to the American landscape and way of life. Between 1932 and 1958, he published three books on the subject of urban planning, the last of which was *The Living City* (Horizon Press, 1958). In his model of Broadacre City, which was exhibited in New York and other major cities, Wright allocated an acre of land to each resident and showed how the contemporary community could be integrated into the natural setting free of the noise, pollution, and crowding of cities. The automobile would be an integral feature, with provision for roadways, parking, and service. An unpublished perspective view of the proposed city includes several of Wright's buildings, among them the Marin County Civic Center and a number of other projects that were not realized. The decentralized city was to shape itself to the contours of a given region, as the civic center does to the low hills of its California site and Taliesin West to its desert mesa. As Anthony Alofsin observes in *Frank Lloyd Wright: Architect* (Museum of Modern Art, 1994): "Broadacre City shared with other modernist visions a set of beliefs in rational solutions to problems of planning. These included a call for central administration, an emphasis on transportation networks, a focus on the machine as a metaphor for industrial technology, and the provision of discrete zones for leisure and work activities."

The top-lighted galleried workspaces of the civic center have their counterpart as early as 1903 in the Larkin Building of Buffalo, New York, which turned inward to shut out a grimy factory neighborhood. More than fifty years after the construction of the Larkin Building, this elegant modernist complex of Marin County looks outward to a setting much closer to the ideal Wright sought for his city of the future. As early as 1932, in *The Disappearing City*, he had written: "Life itself is become the restless 'tenant' in the big city. The citizen himself has lost sight of the true aim of human existence and accepts substitute aims as his life." In opposition to this dehumanizing trend, he proposed a solution that was realized at least in part in his design for Marin County: "New forces openly thrusting at the old form."

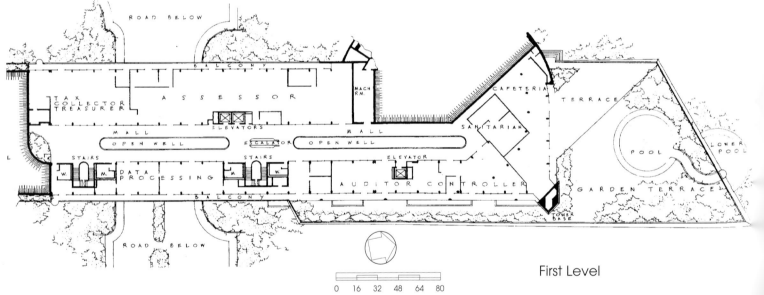

First Level

Interior gallery of Administration Building, first level (Far left)

Space flows over and around the galleries at each level, from which one can look down into the open well to the main level.

Balcony (Right)

Geometric forms in aluminum were used extensively throughout the civic center.

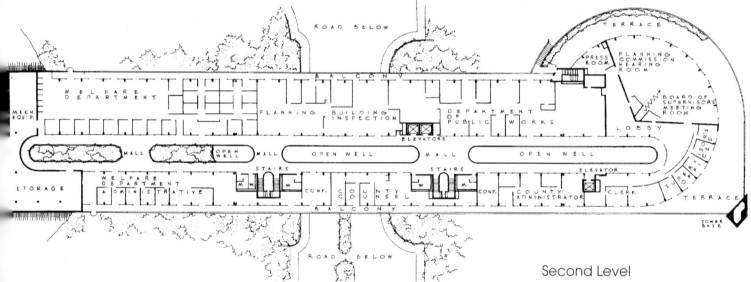

Second Level

Floor plan (Above)

Shown here are two of the four levels of the Administration Building. The entry level is located underneath only the north half of the building. The topmost level is similar in layout to the second level.

Terrace (Left)

The curving lines of the terrace are a counterpoint to the arches which extend the length of the buildings and decrease in size from foundation to roofline.

MARIN COUNTY GO
FRANK LLOYD WRI